TRUE OR FALSE MAZES™ CHRISTMAS SPECIAL!

THE ORIGINAL TRUE OR FALSE MAZES™

BY
SCOTT PETERS

MERRY CHRISTMAS

Prepare for a Festive Maze Adventure!

Greetings, fellow maze explorer! Get ready for a yuletide journey like no other, filled with Christmas magic and maze merriment. Here's how it all works:

Maze Merriment: Flip through the pages and embark on mind-boggling mazes. Your mission? Solve them! But here's the jolly twist - two exits await, and only one leads to holiday cheer.

Guess the Surprise: Before you celebrate victory, take a festive guess. Which exit do you think holds the merry surprise? Trust your instincts and get ready for a Christmas challenge.

Unwrap the Magic: After you've conquered the maze and made your guess, it's time for the big reveal. Did you outsmart the maze and choose the path to holiday happiness? The answer is just a flip away!

Christmas Wonders: But that's not all! Alongside the answers, you'll unwrap delightful Christmas facts that will warm your heart. Learning has never been this jolly!

Enjoy the Festive Journey: Remember, it's not just about reaching the end; it's about the joyful adventure along the way. Embrace the Christmas spirit and let the maze merriment begin!

Get ready to explore, guess, and uncover Christmas truths in the merriest way possible. Are you up for the Christmas challenge?

Cheers to a maze-filled holiday extravaganza!

Wishing you a very happy holiday season,

Scott Peters

TRUE OR FALSE?

Rudolph is one of Santa's original reindeer.

TAKE A WILD GUESS! T ☐ F ☐

FIND OUT!

FALSE

TRUE

Before becoming one of Santa's reindeer, Rudolph was a regular young reindeer, and he was often left out of reindeer games. But one Christmas Eve, Santa asked Rudolph to lead his sleigh because of his glowing nose, and he became famous!

True or False Mazes: Christmas   By Scott Peters

TRUE OR FALSE?
Santa has an official pilot's license.

TAKE A WILD GUESS! T☐ F☐

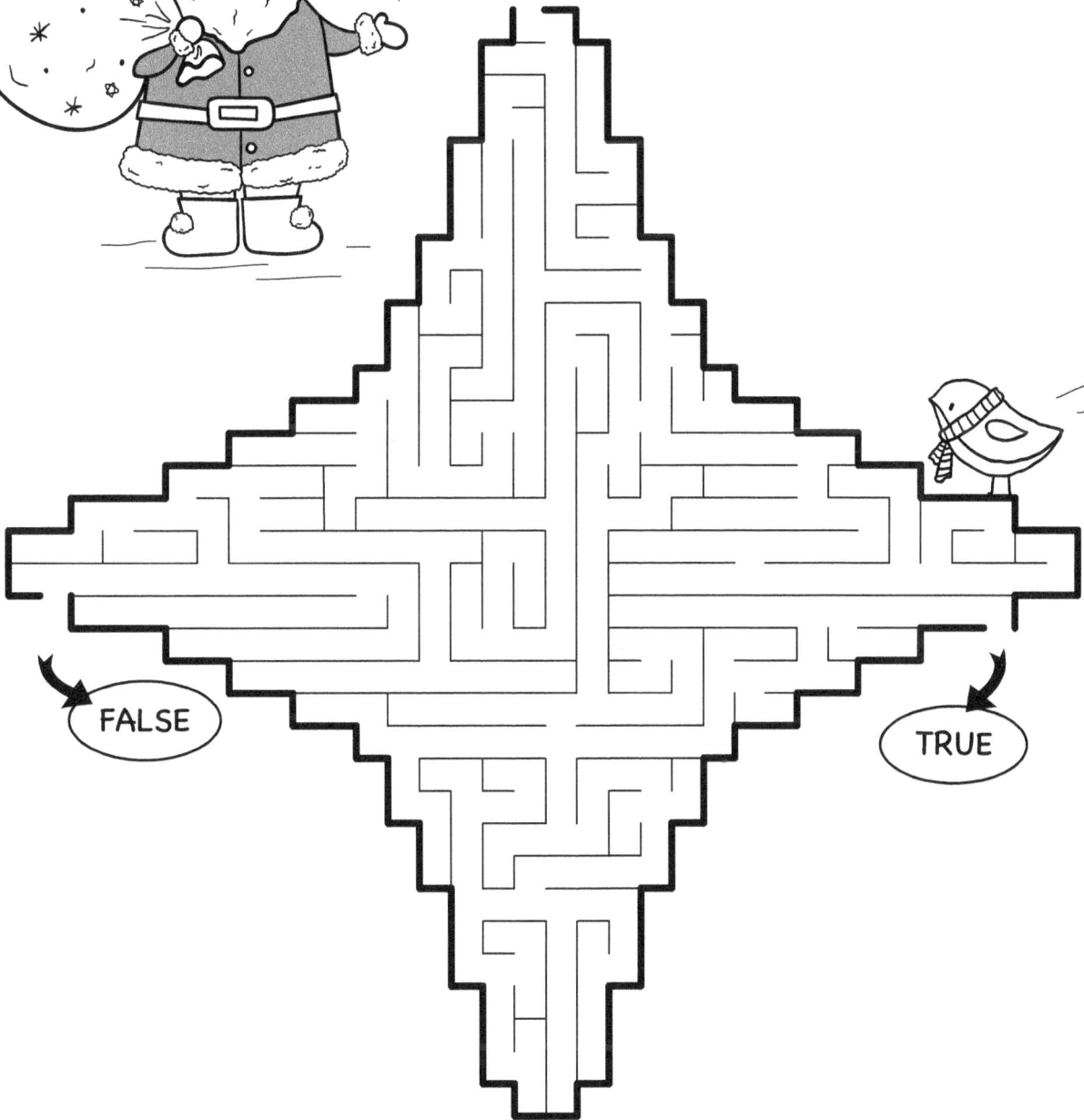

FIND OUT!

FALSE

TRUE

Santa is not just a jolly gift-giver; he's also a licensed pilot! Back in 1927, the U.S. government gave Santa Claus his very own pilot's license. So, he's all set to soar through the skies and spread holiday cheer!

TRUE OR FALSE?

The biggest snowflake measured 5 inches across.

TAKE A WILD GUESS! T☐ F☐

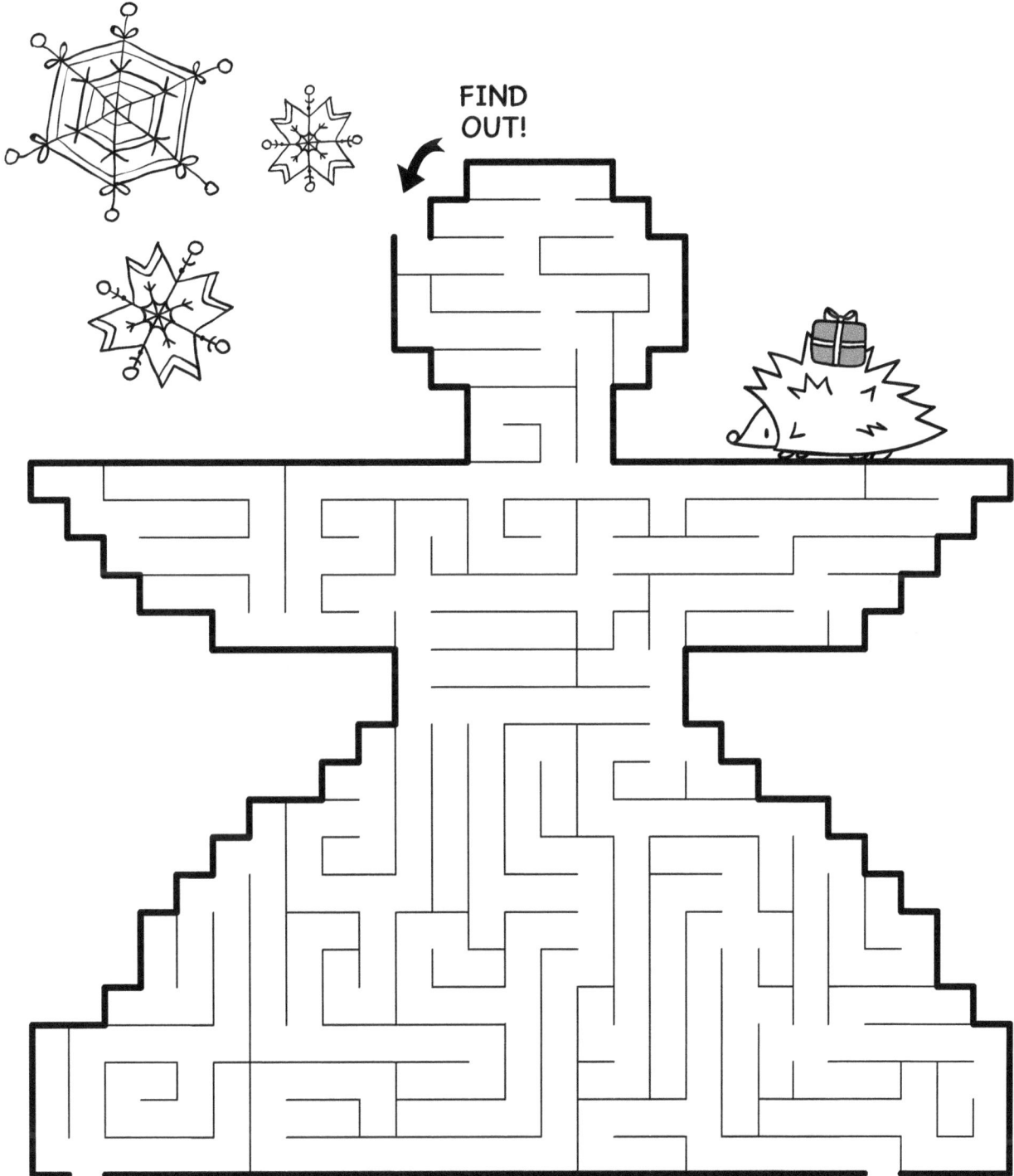

FIND
OUT!

TRUE

FALSE

The biggest snowflake ever recorded was a giant! It measured a massive 15 inches across and 8 inches thick. This super-sized snowflake was found in Fort Keogh, Montana, way back in 1887. Imagine it being like lots of tiny snow crystals huddling together to create one gigantic snowflake!

True or False Mazes: Christmas 💡 By Scott Peters

TRUE OR FALSE?
Tinsel used to be made of real silver.

TAKE A WILD GUESS! T☐ F☐

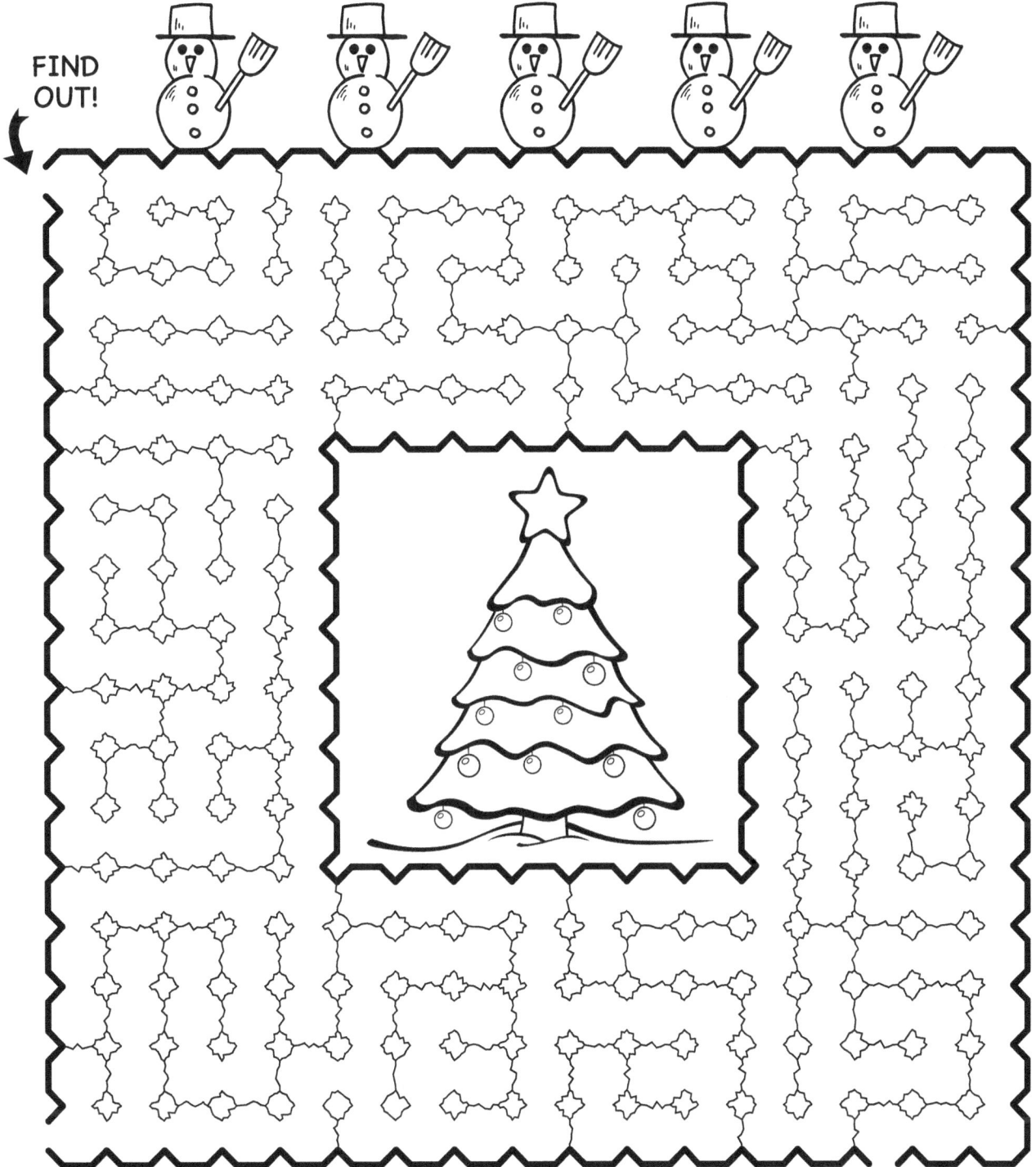

FIND OUT!

FALSE

TRUE

Tinsel is a decoration that looks like shiny ice and is made of thin strips of sparkly material. People sometimes put it on their Christmas trees to make them look even more magical. A long time ago, it was made from real silver, and you can imagine how sparkly it must have been!

TRUE OR FALSE?
Red poinsettia flowers come from Mexico.

TAKE A WILD GUESS! T☐ F☐

FIND
OUT!

TRUE

FALSE

Poinsettias originally come from Mexico. They're named after Joel Poinsett, who was the first U.S. ambassador to Mexico in the 1820s. He saw the beautiful red and green plants there and brought them back to the United States. Poinsettias became popular for Christmas because of their festive colors, and they bloom during the holiday season.

True or False Mazes: Christmas By Scott Peters

TRUE OR FALSE?

Scrooge is visited by three ghosts.

TAKE A WILD GUESS! T☐ F☐

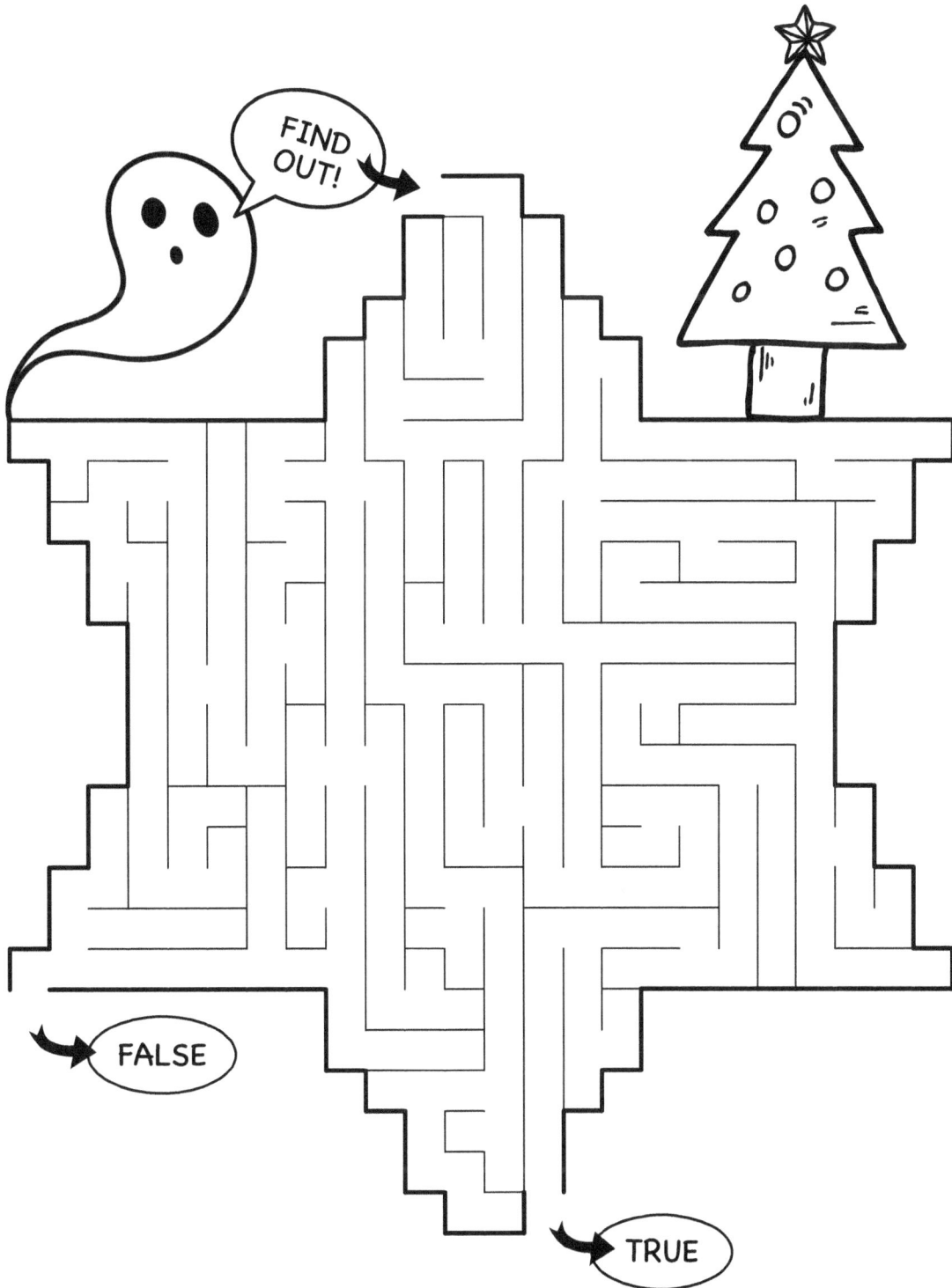

FIND OUT!

FALSE

TRUE

In A Christmas Carol, Scrooge is a grumpy, selfish man who doesn't like Christmas. He's visited by four ghosts: Jacob Marley, the Ghost of Christmas Past, the Ghost of Christmas Present, and the Ghost of Christmas Yet to Come. They help him see the importance of love and generosity during the holiday season.

True or False Mazes: Christmas   By Scott Peters

TRUE OR FALSE?

People invented wreaths over 2,000 years ago.

TAKE A WILD GUESS! T ☐ F ☐

FIND OUT!

TRUE

FALSE

Wreaths have a long history! People started making them as crowns in 8th century BC when Etruscan rulers wore wreaths to show off their achievements or status. The Romans and Greece; people used wreaths too. Ancient Rome had special meanings. The types of plants used in wreaths symbolize wisdom. According to mythology, Zeus sat under an oak tree so oak wreaths symbolize wisdom.

True or False Mazes: Christmas 💡 By Scott Peters

TRUE OR FALSE?

'Silent Night' was originally written in English.

TAKE A WILD GUESS! T☐ F☐

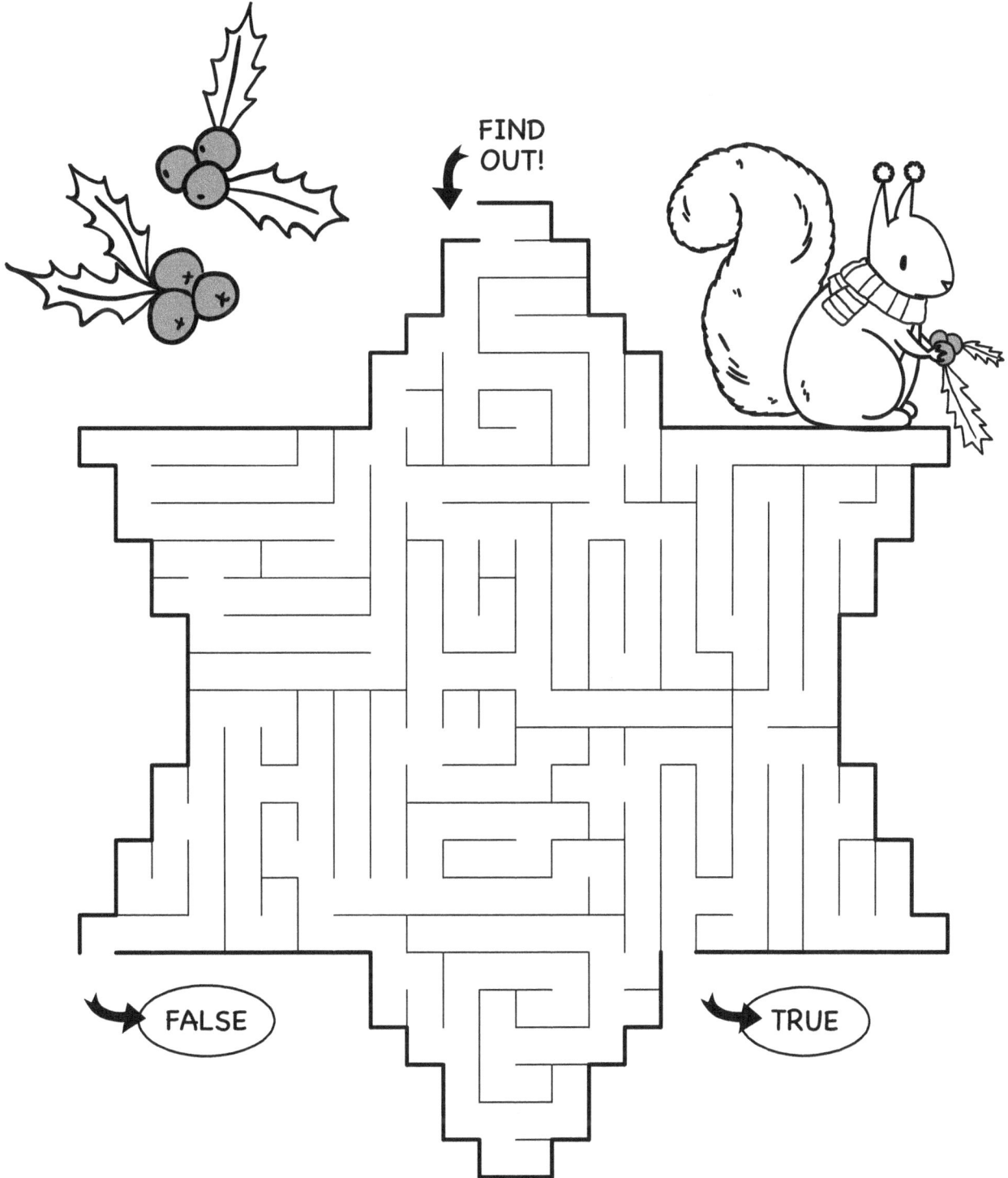

FIND OUT!

FALSE

TRUE

"Silent Night" is a Christmas song that was written over a hundred years ago in the German language. The very first words of the song are "Stille Nacht, heilige Nacht." People sing it all over the world during Christmas to celebrate the holiday.

TRUE OR FALSE?

Most British people eat turkey on Christmas day.

TAKE A WILD GUESS! T☐ F☐

FIND OUT!

EXTRA HARD!

TRUE

FALSE

In the UK, turkey is a star on Christmas dinner tables, even though these birds came from far away in the 16th century! Back then, even folks used to feast on geese, boar, and sometimes even fancy peacocks before they made turkey the Christmas superstar.

True or False Mazes: Christmas 💡 By Scott Peters

TRUE OR FALSE?

Frosty the Snowman always has 4 fingers.

TAKE A WILD GUESS! T ☐ F ☐

FIND
OUT!

FALSE

TRUE

Here's a fun fact! In the cartoon special Frosty the snowman usually animated with four fingers, just enough to count to five. But in one quick moment he's when he tries to count, the video around the 48-second mark!

TRUE OR FALSE?

Candy canes were originally straight.

TAKE A WILD GUESS! T☐ F☐

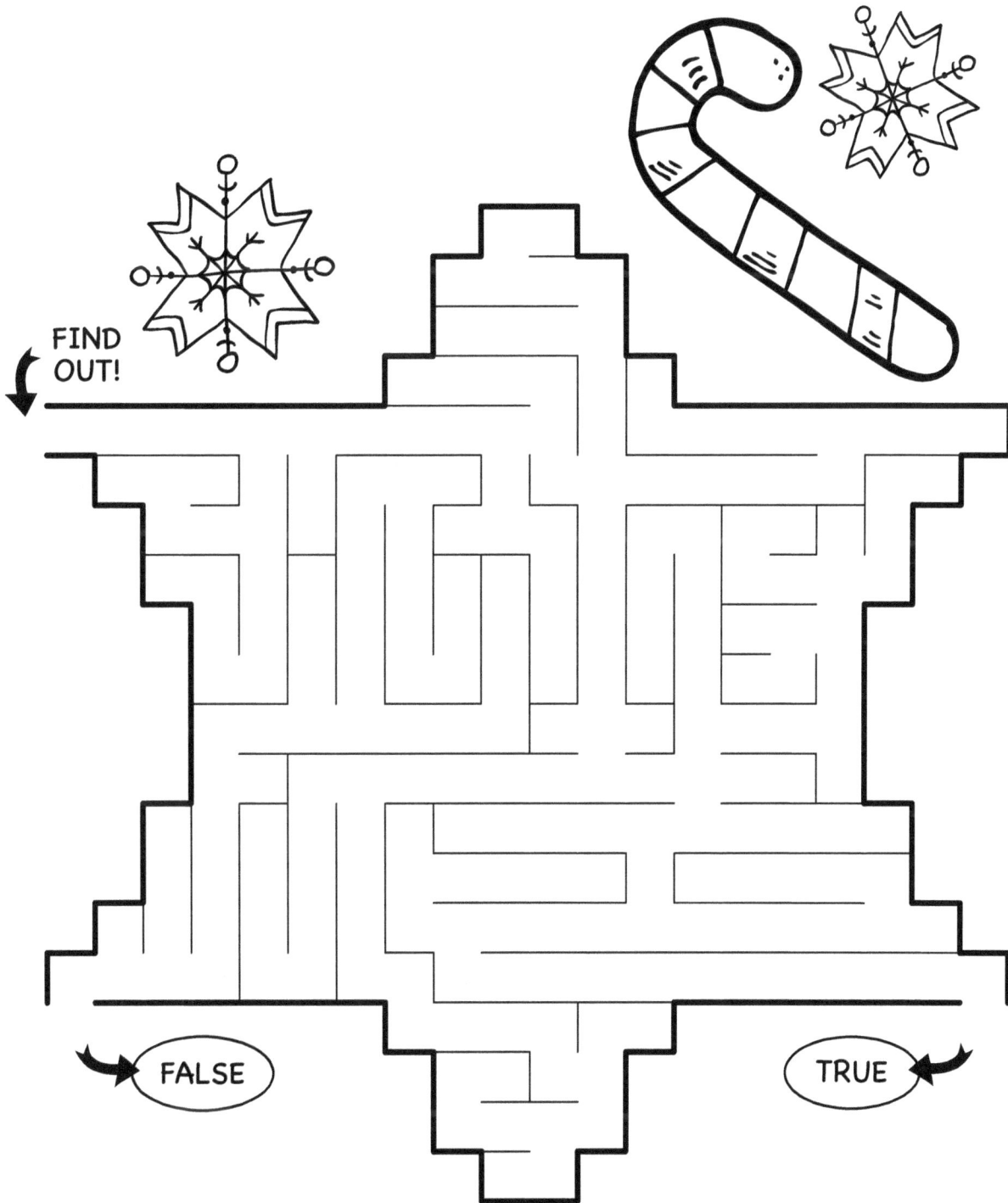

FIND OUT!

FALSE

TRUE

Candy canes used to be straight sticks of candy. But later, someone had a clever idea to bend them into a curve, like a shepherd's crook or cane. As a bonus, they're perfect for hanging on Christmas tree branches!

TRUE OR FALSE?
Reindeer can't swim.

TAKE A WILD GUESS! T☐ F☐

TRUE

FALSE

Reindeer! They also known as caribou in some places, are excellent swimmers! They can paddle at speeds of 4 to 6 miles per hour using their big hooves like flippers. Their hollow fur helps them stay afloat, and they often have to swim across large rivers during migration!

True or False Mazes: Christmas ☀ By Scott Peters

TRUE OR FALSE?

Tom Hanks played 6 roles in 'The Polar Express.'

TAKE A WILD GUESS! T☐ F☐

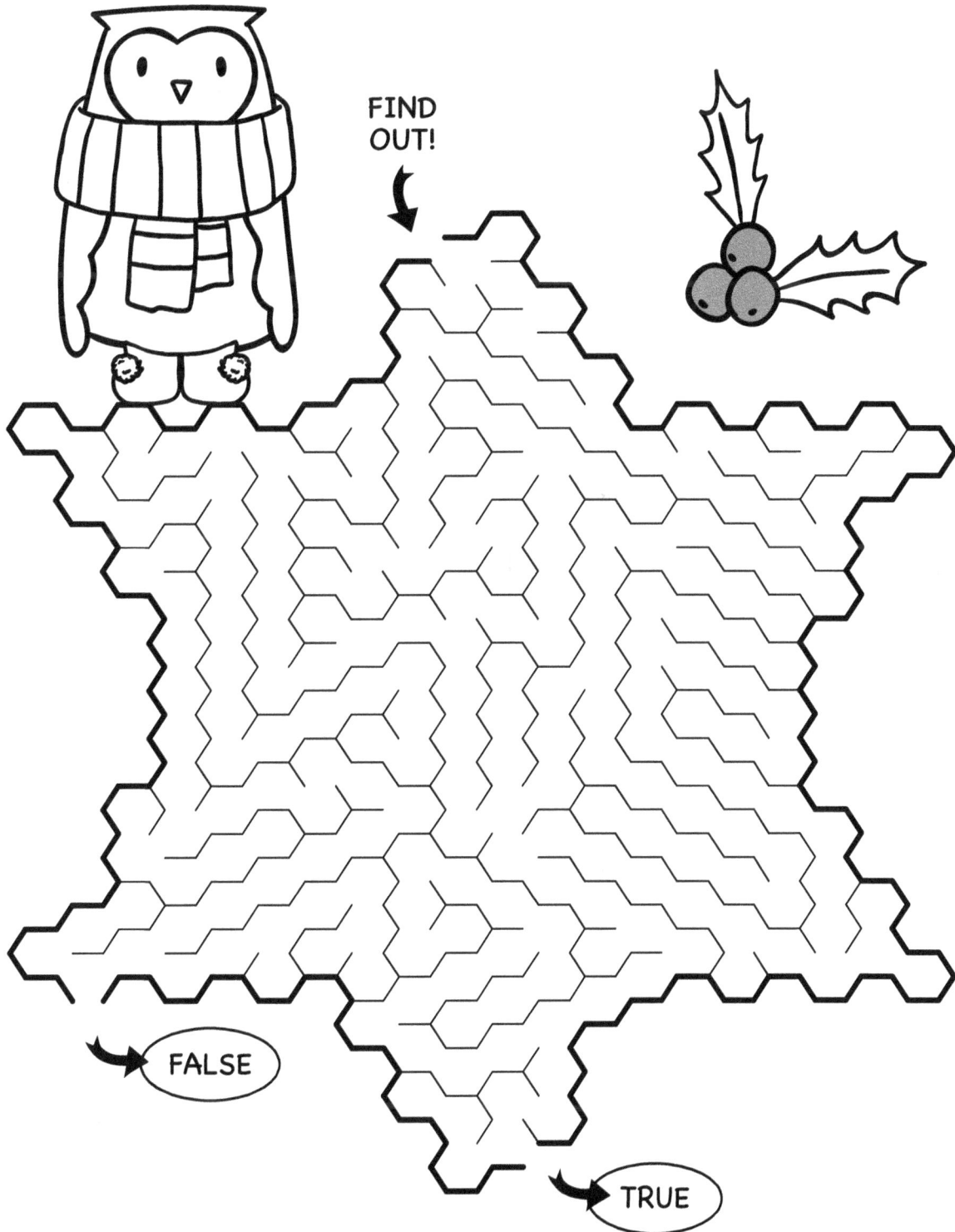

FIND OUT!

FALSE

TRUE

Tom Hanks didn't just hop on 'The Polar Express' once, he hopped on six times! He didn't even need a magic ticket, or all! He also stepped into the shoes (or voices) of Hero Boy, the voice of the conductor, and that's not all! He also Father, Hobo, Scrooge, and even Santa Claus.

TRUE OR FALSE?

There's a basketball court sized gingerbread house.

TAKE A WILD GUESS! T☐ F☐

FIND OUT!

TRUE   FALSE

In Bryan, Texas, there's a gigantic gingerbread house that's as big as a basketball court! Baking enthusiast Cheryl Kirchen built it in 2013, and it's a whopping 2,520 square feet. Imagine a house made of 6 million pieces of gingerbread, 12,000 candy canes, 600 pounds of icing, and over 10,000 twinkling lights!

True or False Mazes: Christmas   By Scott Peters

TRUE OR FALSE?
Most people buy real Christmas trees.

TAKE A WILD GUESS! T☐ F☐

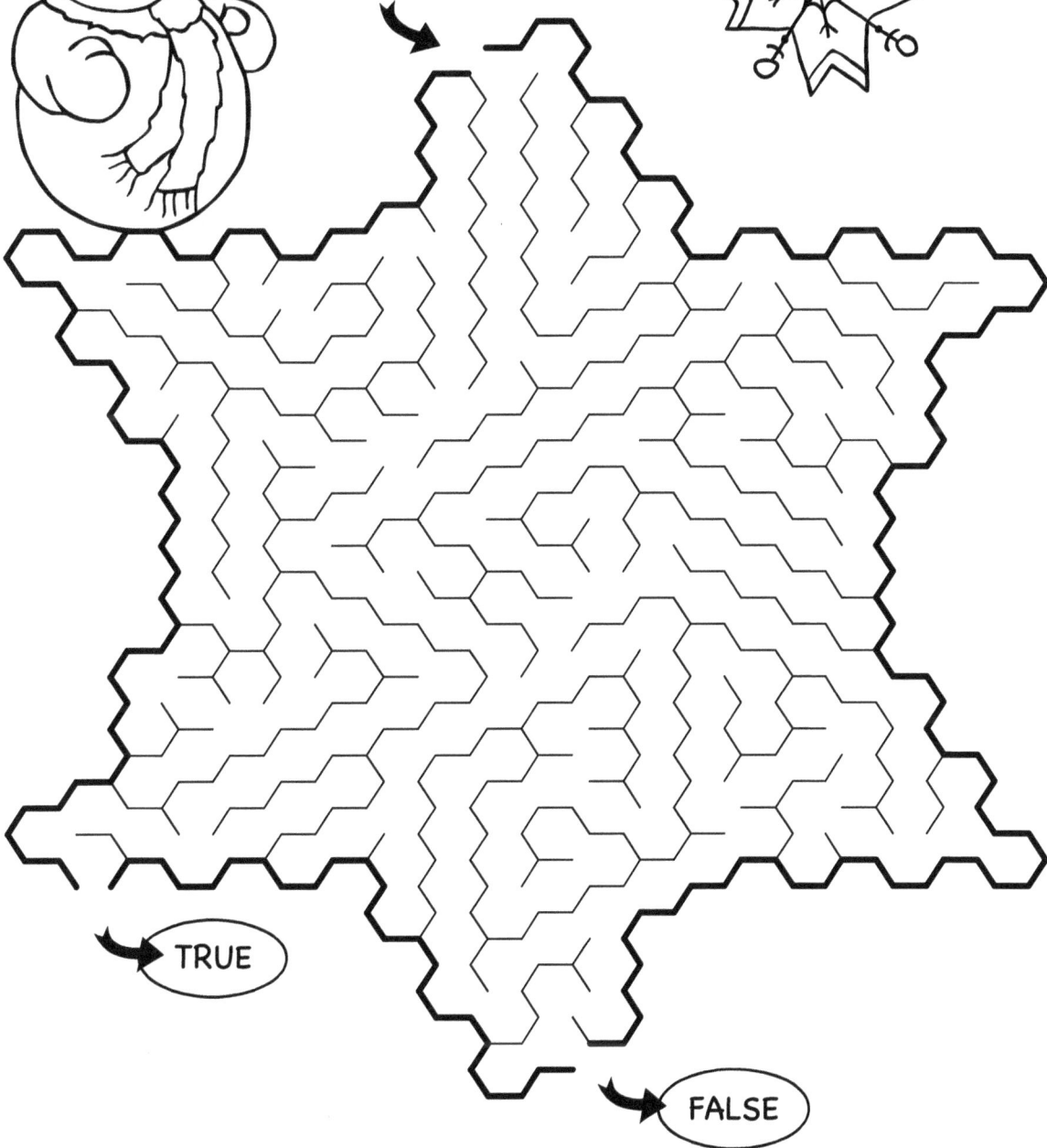

FIND OUT!

TRUE

FALSE

Whoa, in 2020, nearly 94 million homes in the U.S. had a Christmas tree! But guess what? A whopping 85 percent of those trees were the artificial kind. Looks like many folks went for the reusable sparkle!

TRUE OR FALSE?

It's a Japanese tradition to eat KFC for Christmas.

TAKE A WILD GUESS! T ☐ F ☐

FIND OUT!

TRUE

FALSE

TRUE OR FALSE?

Grab a pencil and make your way through the maze.

Hey, did you know that around 3.6 million families in Japan have a holiday season has become a nationwide thing in Japan! enjoying some Kentucky Fried Chicken during the campaign in 1974 called "Kentucky for Christmas." Now, tasty Christmas tradition? It all began with a clever marketing

True or False Mazes: Christmas 💡 By Scott Peters

TRUE OR FALSE?

The tallest cut Christmas tree was 240 feet.

TAKE A WILD GUESS! T☐ F☐

FIND
OUT!

TRUE

FALSE

Close! The tallest Christmas tree ever cut was seriously sky-high, standing at a jaw-dropping 221 feet tall! That's taller than a 20-story building, and they decked out this towering Douglas fir with all the festive trimmings at a shopping center in Seattle back in 1950, as confirmed by Guinness World Records.

True or False Mazes: Christmas 💡 By Scott Peters

TRUE OR FALSE?

Jingle Bells was the first song played in space.

TAKE A WILD GUESS! T☐ F☐

FIND OUT!

FALSE

TRUE

TRUE OR FALSE?

Santa has his own zip code (postal code) in Canada.

TAKE A WILD GUESS! T ☐ F ☐

FIND OUT!

TRUE

FALSE

Guess what? Santa Claus has his own special zip code in Canada! It's HOH OHO! Santa Claus can actually send letters to Santa at this address: Santa Claus, North Pole, HOH OHO, Canada! And here's the magical part—some very lucky kids receive letters back from Santa letter program!

True or False Mazes: Christmas 💡 By Scott Peters

TRUE OR FALSE?

There are 200 gifts in the '12 Days of Christmas' song.

TAKE A WILD GUESS! T ☐ F ☐

FIND OUT!

TRUE

FALSE

Imagine this: If you decided to give all the gifts from the song "The Twelve Days of Christmas," you'd be handing out a whopping 364 presents! That's almost enough gifts to cover every single day of the year.

True or False Mazes: Christmas   By Scott Peters

TRUE OR FALSE?

Santa's sleigh is the fastest vehicle in the world.

TAKE A WILD GUESS! T☐ F☐

FIND OUT!

TRUE

FALSE

Santa's sleigh is like a super-speedy rocket! On Christmas Eve, Santa zips around the globe to bring gifts to all the kids. There are about 2.5 billion children on his list, so his sleigh has to zoom at an astonishing 1,800 miles per second. That's faster than lightning!

True or False Mazes: Christmas   By Scott Peters

TRUE OR FALSE?

Most Americans celebrate Christmas.

TAKE A WILD GUESS! T☐ F☐

TRUE OR FALSE?

Joy to the World is the best selling Christmas song.

TAKE A WILD GUESS! T☐ F☐

FIND OUT!

FALSE

TRUE

True or False Mazes: Christmas   By Scott Peters

TRUE OR FALSE?

A handmade doll was the first Toys for Tots donation.

TAKE A WILD GUESS! T ☐ F ☐

FIND OUT!

FALSE

TRUE

Toys for Tots started in 1947 was a hit with made the grand entrance generous folks. And guess who donated by first toy drive in sunny Los Angeles, California. Their very as the very first donation? A lovely handmade doll!

True or False Mazes: Christmas By Scott Peters

TRUE OR FALSE?

Santa's elves have nothing to do all summer long.

TAKE A WILD GUESS! T ☐ F ☐

FIND
OUT!

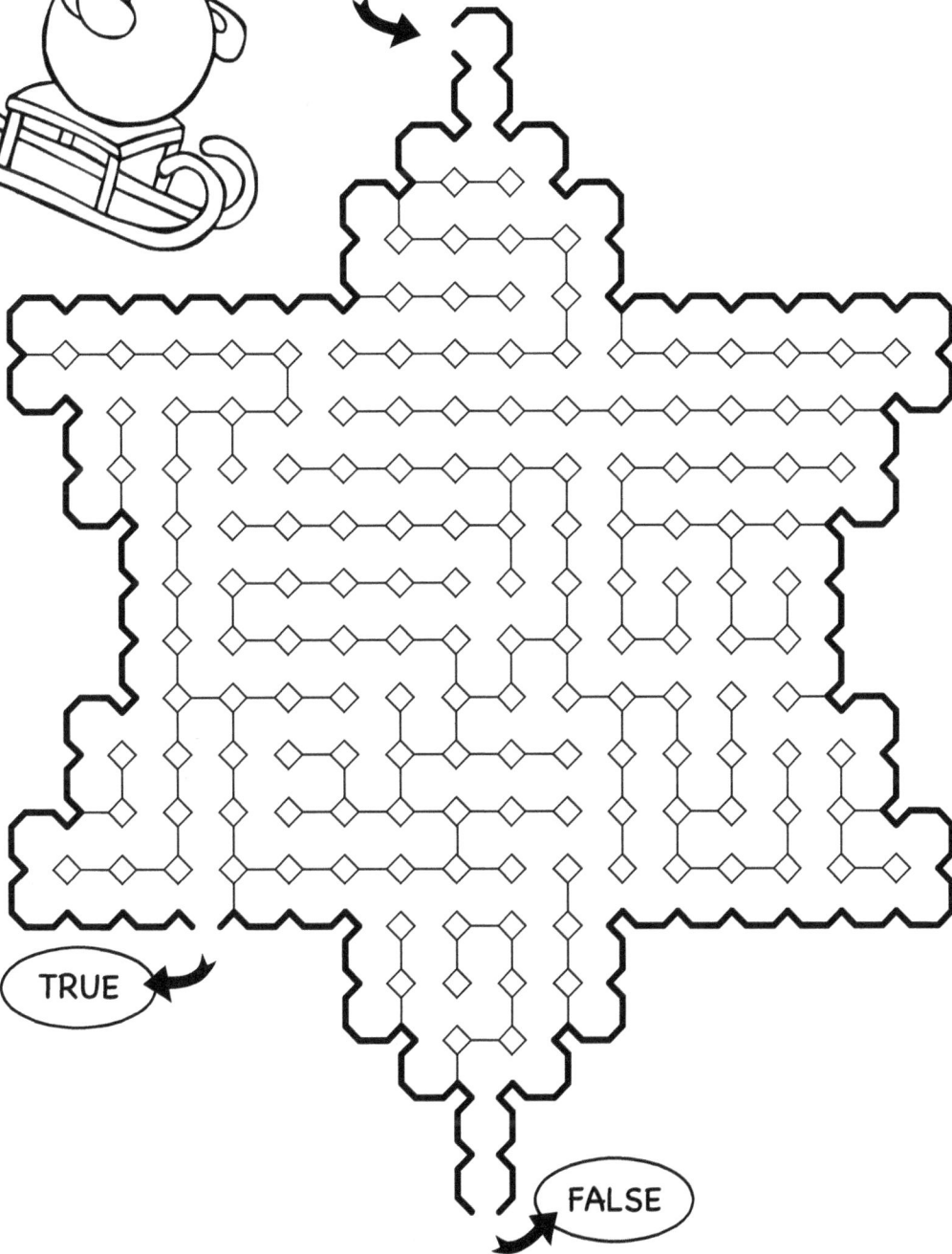

TRUE

FALSE

Santa's workshop is buzzing with activity all year long! While the exact number of elves is a secret, they pour their hearts into creating wonderful gifts for children around the world.

TRUE OR FALSE?

Franklin Pierce was the first U.S. President
to put up a tree.

TAKE A WILD GUESS! T ☐ F ☐

FIND OUT!

TRUE

FALSE

Franklin Pierce, the 14th president of the United States, was the trailblazer who graced the White House with its first official Christmas tree in the year 1856. Nowadays, the White House turns into a festive wonderland with lots of decorations, special ornaments, and fun celebrations. It's a big part of how the U.S. gets into the holiday spirit.

True or False Mazes: Christmas   By Scott Peters

TRUE OR FALSE?

Grown ups did all the voices for 'A Charlie Brown Christmas.'

TAKE A WILD GUESS! T ☐ F ☐

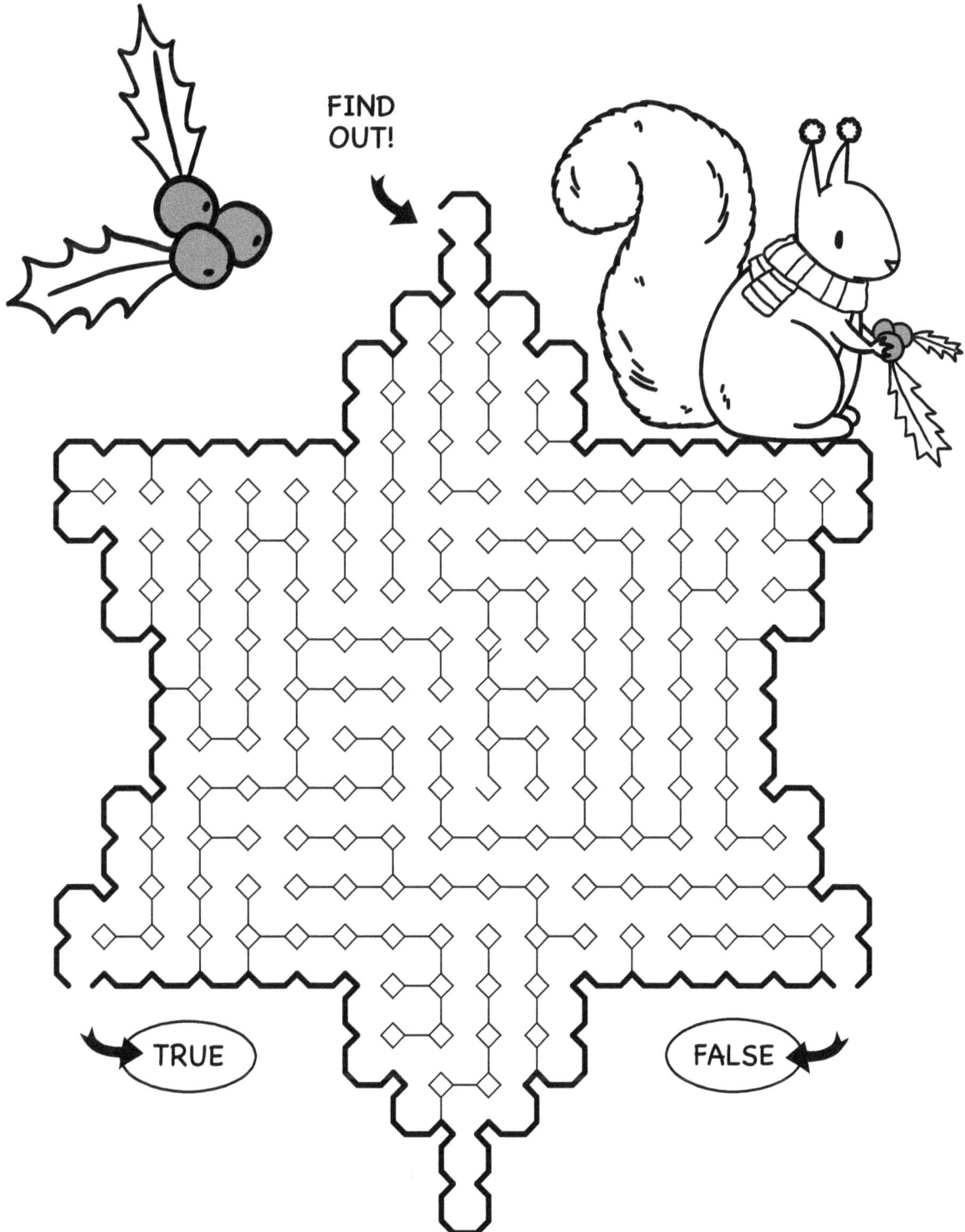

FIND OUT!

TRUE

FALSE

For A Charlie Brown Christmas, the creator, Charles Schulz, wanted real kids as actors. But here's the twist: some of them were so young that they couldn't read the script. So, the team had to help them by reciting the lines one by one, voiced by Christopher Shea. Linus, even for

True or False Mazes: Christmas 💡 By Scott Peters

TRUE OR FALSE?

Queen Elizabeth invented gingerbread men.

TAKE A WILD GUESS! T☐ F☐

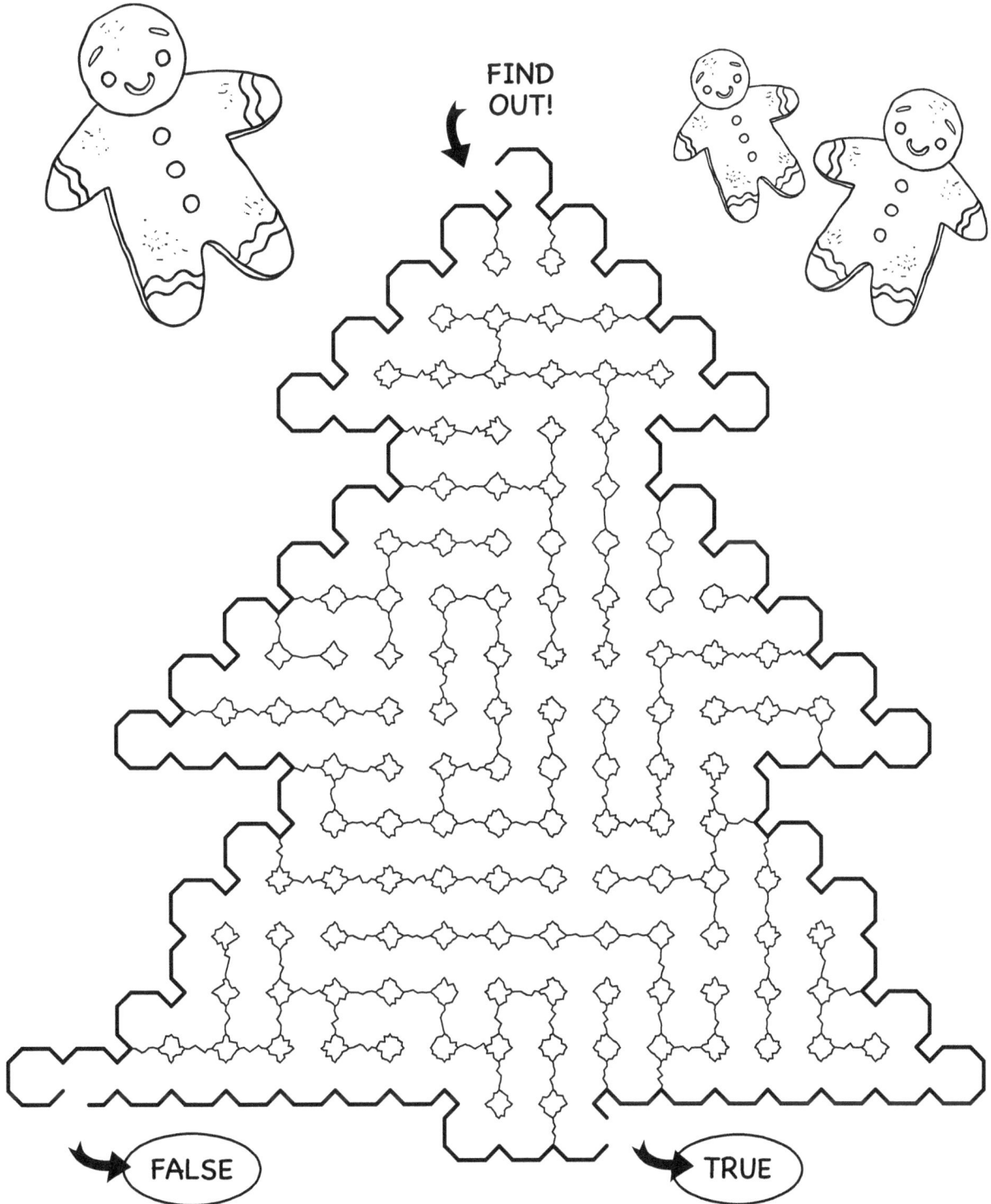

FIND OUT!

FALSE

TRUE

TRUE or FALSE?

Elizabeth invented gingerbread men.

Queen Elizabeth gets the credit for inventing gingerbread men!
She had a clever idea: she asked her cook to make
gingerbread cookies that looked like her important guests
and friends. It was her sweet way of honoring them.

True or False Mazes: Christmas 💡 By Scott Peters

TRUE OR FALSE?

In Australia, Christmas is in summertime.

TAKE A WILD GUESS! T ☐ F ☐

FIND OUT!

FALSE

TRUE

Christmas in Australia

Since Australia is unlike the snowy scenes you might imagine, December! Australia is located below the equator, it's summer in So instead of snowflakes and chilly weather, Australians celebrate with sunshine, barbecues, and trips to the beach. Santa might even trade in his reindeer for a surfboard!

True or False Mazes: Christmas   By Scott Peters

TRUE OR FALSE?

There's no such thing as a Yule Goat.

TAKE A WILD GUESS! T☐ F☐

FIND
OUT!

TRUE

FALSE

In Sweden, they've got a unique Christmas tradition with the Yule Goat, dating back to the 11th century. It used to be Santa's sidekick and was said to ride the Yule Goat to give out Christmas ornament or made of straw all over Sweden. Nowadays, you'll see the Yule Goat as a cute Christmas ornament or made of straw all over Sweden.

TRUE OR FALSE?

Ukrainians hang spiderwebs on their Christmas trees.

TAKE A WILD GUESS! T☐ F☐

FALSE

TRUE

In Ukraine, a unique Christmas tree legend has it that a poor widow adorned her tree with spider webs. Legend has it that a beautiful web of silver and gold, overnight, it transformed into a beautiful web of silver and gold, delighting her children. To bring good luck, Ukrainians now hang spider web-shaped ornaments on their trees.

True or False Mazes: Christmas By Scott Peters

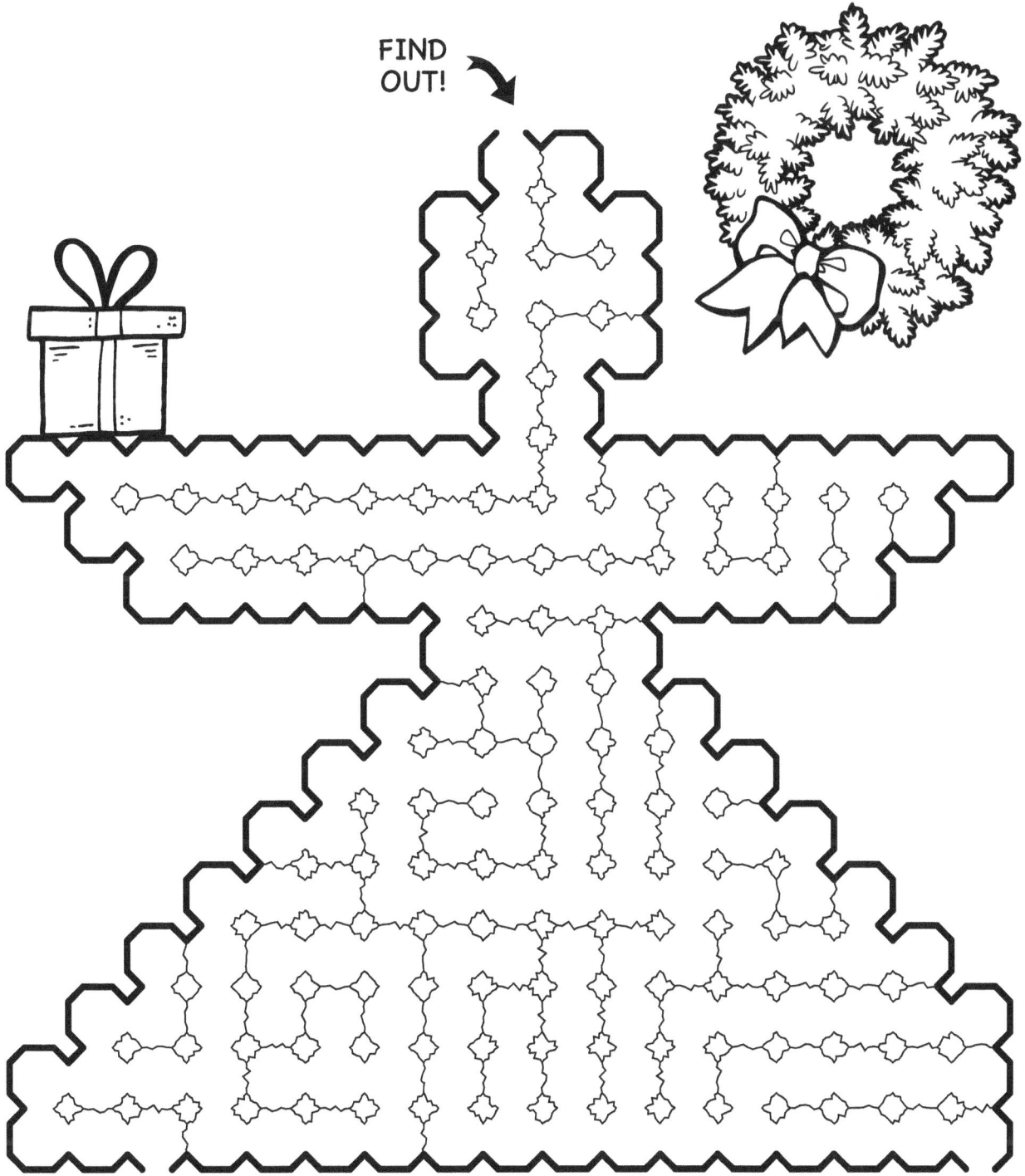

TRUE OR FALSE?
Germany has a Christmas pickle.

TAKE A WILD GUESS! T☐ F☐

FIND OUT!

FALSE

TRUE

In Germany, they add a fun twist to Christmas trees by hiding a pickle ornament in the branches. The first child to find it gets a special present. Some believe the pickle is a centuries-old tradition, others believe it's because a pickle once saved a hungry soldier from starving to death on Christmas Eve.

True or False Mazes: Christmas   By Scott Peters

TRUE OR FALSE?

In Norway, people hide brooms on Christmas Eve.

TAKE A WILD GUESS! T ☐ F ☐

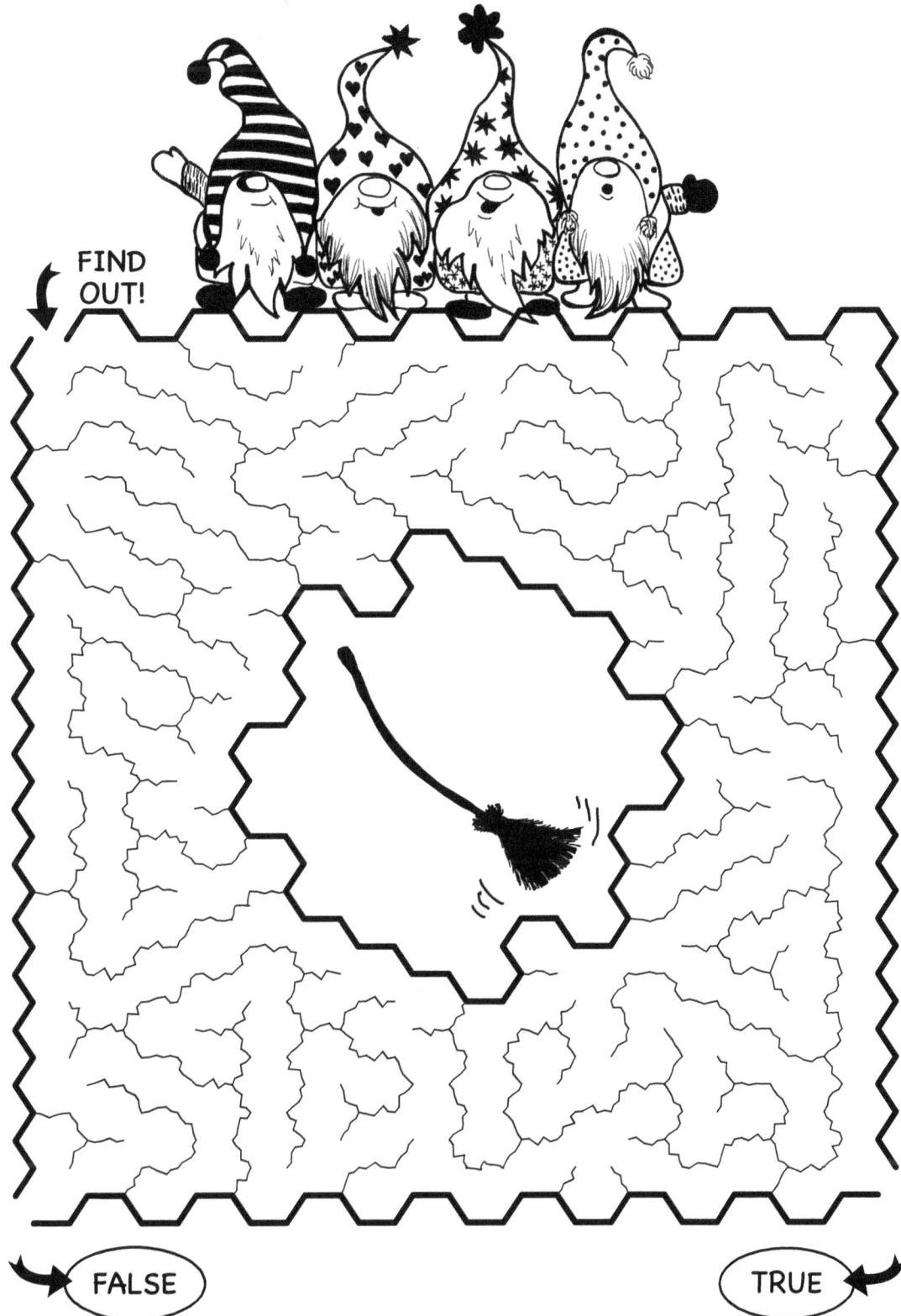

FIND OUT!

FALSE

TRUE

Norwegians have a quirky Christmas tradition: they believe that they hide their brooms on Christmas Eve. Why? Well, they come out to play on this night, and if they spot a broom, they might take it for a midnight ride! Mischievous spirits and witches

True or False Mazes: Christmas 💡 By Scott Peters

TRUE OR FALSE?

Traditional Christmas cards are losing their popularity.

TAKE A WILD GUESS! T ☐ F ☐

FIND OUT!

FALSE

TRUE

Believe it or not, a staggering 1.6 billion Christmas cards are sent in the U.S. every year! Millennials are big fans of greeting cards. They're responsible for nearly 20 percent of the money spent on them, and their love for cards is growing faster than any other generation's. So, it looks like sending heartfelt wishes on paper isn't going away anytime soon!

TRUE OR FALSE?

President Jackson held a snowball fight in the White House

TAKE A WILD GUESS! T ☐ F ☐

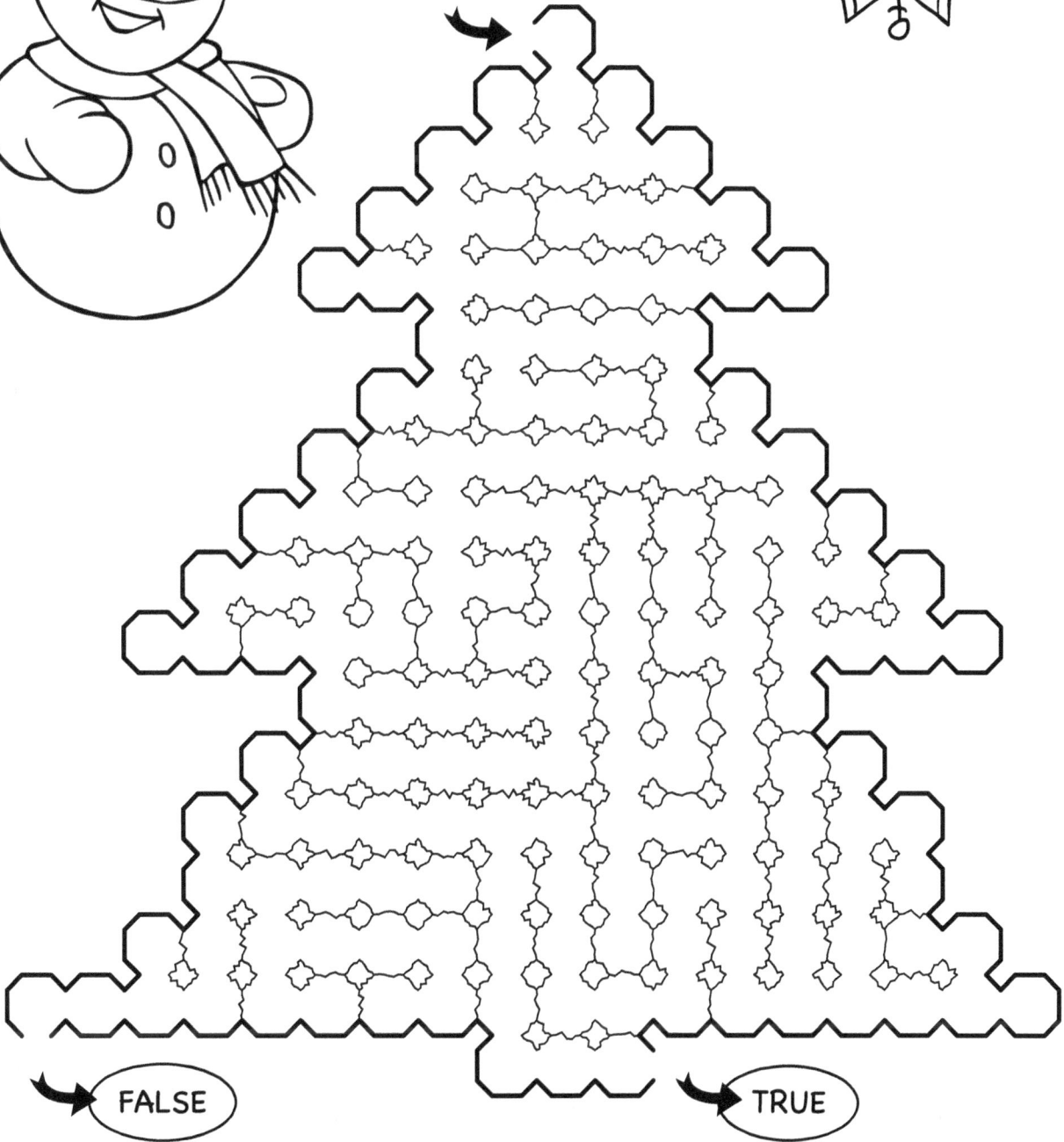

FIND OUT!

FALSE

TRUE

In 1834, President Andrew Jackson hosted a grand Christmas party at the White House for his children and grandchildren. The festivities included games, dancing, a lavish dinner, and the main event: an indoor "snowball fight," using specially made cotton balls.

TRUE OR FALSE?

In the fairytale, a bird eats the gingerbread man.

TAKE A WILD GUESS! T☐ F☐

FIND OUT!

FALSE

TRUE

"The Gingerbread Man " is a story about a gingerbread cookie that magically comes to life. This cookie goes on an exciting adventure, trying his wits to outsmart an elderly couple and many animals using his wits to catch him. However, in the end, he faces a clever fox who tricks him and catches him for a tasty snack. It's a tale of excitement with a surprising ending.

True or False Mazes: Christmas   By Scott Peters

TRUE OR FALSE?

There's no such thing as a Christmas Witch.

TAKE A WILD GUESS! T ☐ F ☐

FIND OUT!

TRUE

FALSE

In Italy, Christmas is extra special because they celebrate two gift-giving events! On Christmas Eve, Santa Claus visits the children, but the fun doesn't stop there. On January 5, the night before the Epiphany, a friendly witch named Befana comes bearing gifts. Legend has it that she missed giving baby Jesus a gift, so she makes up for it by delivering presents to all the kids.

True or False Mazes: Christmas   By Scott Peters

TRUE OR FALSE?

Christmas is the most popular day to get engaged.

TAKE A WILD GUESS! T☐ F☐

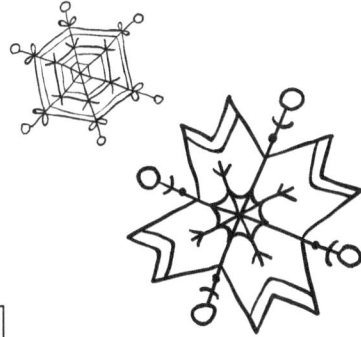

FIND OUT!

TRUE

FALSE

True or False Mazes: Christmas   By Scott Peters

TRUE OR FALSE?

The Grinch is the highest earning Christmas movie.

TAKE A WILD GUESS! T☐ F☐

FIND OUT!

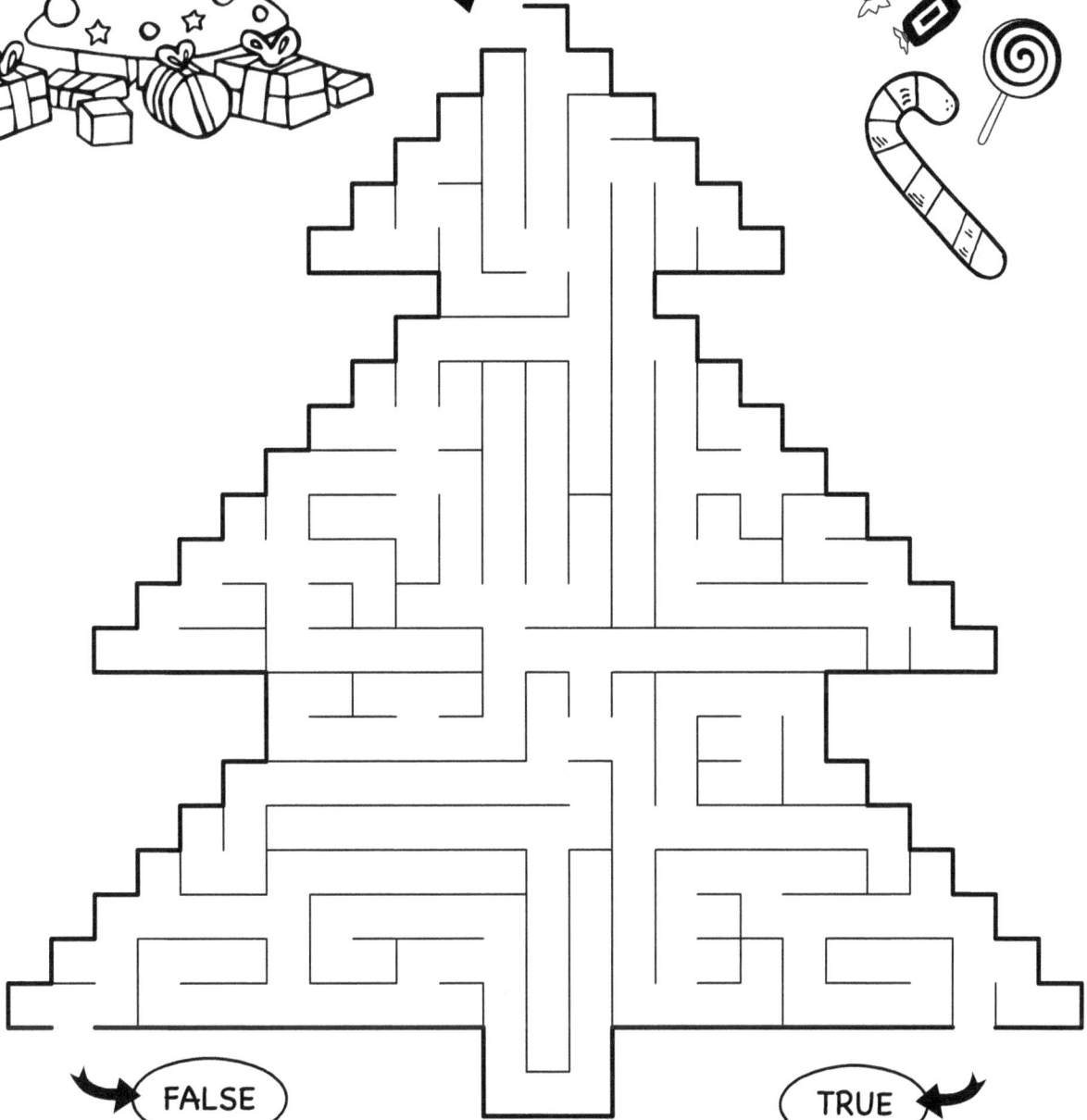

FALSE

TRUE

The 2018 movie "The Grinch" stole the show when it comes to earnings. It raked in a massive $512.9 million in just four years, making it the highest-earning Christmas movie of all time. Until then, Home Alone held the crown. So, it looks like the Grinch isn't just stealing Christmas, but also the top spot in holiday movie earnings!

TRUE OR FALSE?

Mincemeat dessert originally contained meat.

TAKE A WILD GUESS! T☐ F☐

SUPER HARD!

FIND OUT!

TRUE   FALSE

Mincemeat is a festive filling used in pies and desserts during the holiday season. It's a mixture of chopped fruits like apples and raisins, spices, sugar, and sometimes a splash of brandy or rum. In the past, mincemeat did include meat, but over time, it evolved into a sweet and spicy concoction, making it a beloved holiday tradition.

TRUE OR FALSE?

The largest elf gathering was at the South Pole.

TAKE A WILD GUESS! T ☐ F ☐

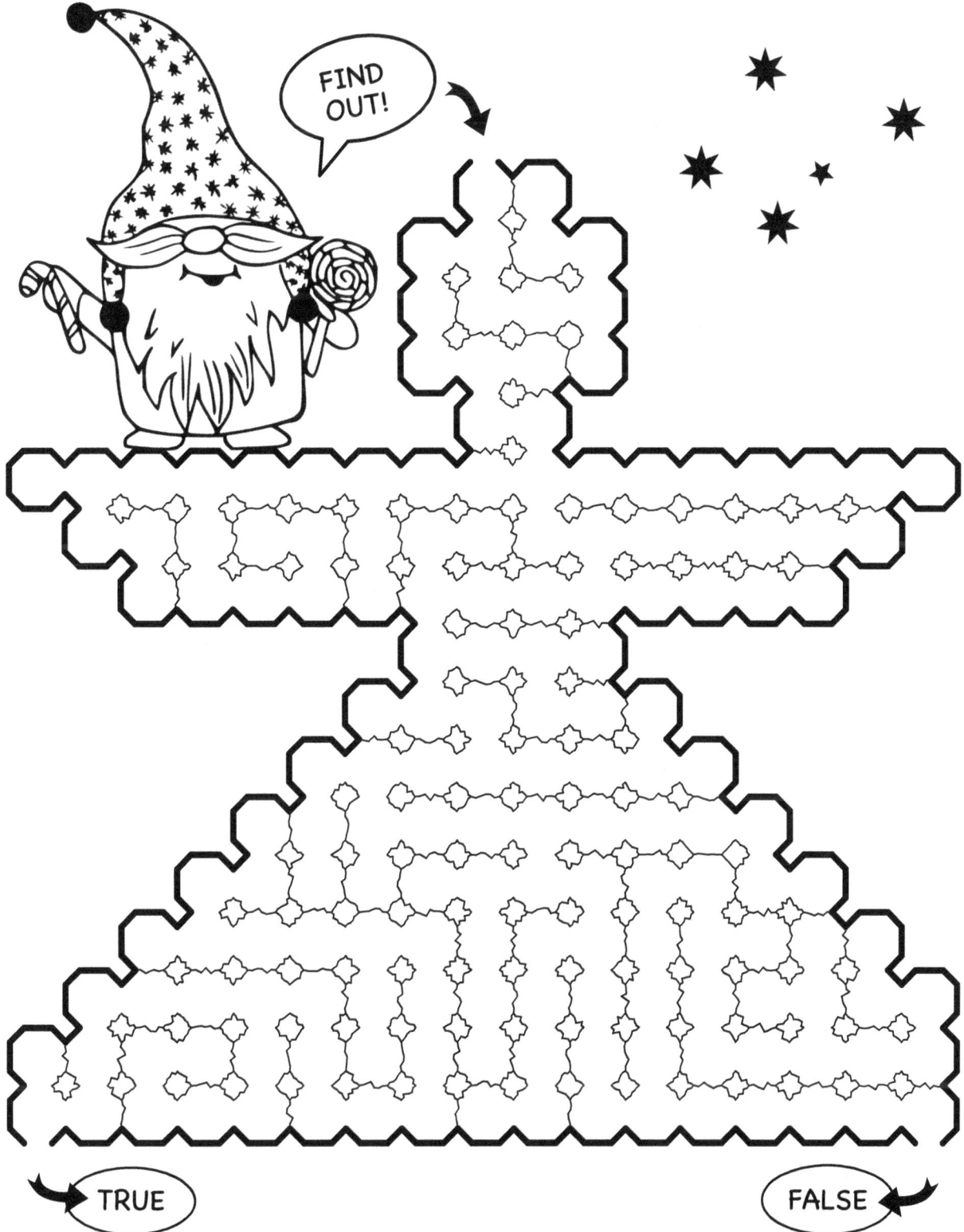

FIND OUT!

TRUE

FALSE

Santa's little helpers: those hardworking elves, usually spend their days crafting in Bangkok, Thailand. But in 2014, they took a break about a month before Christmas. Guess what? They set a record! A whopping 1,762 elves got together, making it the largest gathering of Santa's elves ever.

True or False Mazes: Christmas   By Scott Peters

TRUE OR FALSE?

Those silver balls on cookies are made of real silver.

TAKE A WILD GUESS! T ☐   F ☐

FIND OUT!

FALSE

TRUE

Hold on to your holiday cookies! Those shiny silver sugar pearls might look tempting, but here's the scoop: the FDA doesn't give them the green light for eating because of their silver content. Most states let them be sold, but they're labeled as "for decoration only," not as something to munch on. So, while they make your treats sparkle, it's best not to snack on them!

TRUE OR FALSE?
Elfapalooza is a real thing.

TAKE A WILD GUESS! T☐ F☐

FIND OUT!

TRUE

FALSE

The people of Mobile, Alabama, are on a mission to break the record for the largest gathering of Santa's elves in the world. That's why they host Elfapalooza every year. It's a super fun karaoke event where American elves come together, sing hold an elf march! to find the best elf, and

True or False Mazes: Christmas By Scott Peters

TRUE OR FALSE?

Tumbleweed Christmas trees are common in many states.

TAKE A WILD GUESS! T☐ F☐

FIND OUT!

FALSE

TRUE

TRUE OR FALSE?

Cookies were invented as a portable dessert.

TAKE A WILD GUESS! T ☐   F ☐

FIND OUT!

FALSE

TRUE

You won't believe this fun fact: cookies weren't initially made for munching! They were originally used to test the oven temperature before baking a cake. Back in the day, bakers would grab a small scoop of cake batter and pop it in the oven to see if it realized cookies are delicious on their own! I guess they quickly

True or False Mazes: Christmas   By Scott Peters

TRUE OR FALSE?

Elephants love snacking on Christmas trees.

TAKE A WILD GUESS! T☐ F☐

EXTRA HARD!

FIND OUT!

FALSE

TRUE

Once the holiday fun is over, your Christmas tree has some interesting options. Sure, you could leave it by the curb for the garbage collectors, but how about this: you can also donate it to a zoo! Some zoos, like The Elephant Sanctuary in Tennessee, gladly accept these trees. Why, you ask? Well, the giant herbivores there love chomping on evergreens as a tasty seasonal snack. Your tree could become a treat for a happy elephant!

TRUE OR FALSE?

Holiday decorating is perfectly safe.

TAKE A WILD GUESS! T☐ F☐

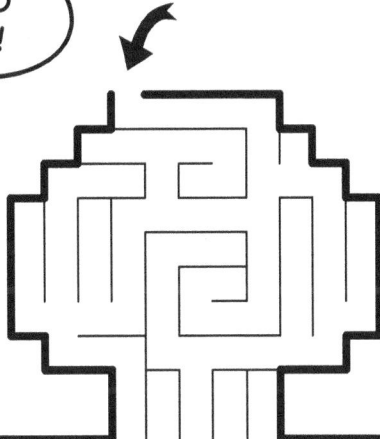

EXTRA HARD!

FIND OUT!

TRUE

FALSE

Decking the halls is fun, but it's important to stay safe! Thousands of folks end up in the ER each year with decorating mishaps. So, make sure in 2018 alone, a whopping 17,500 people had to visit the hospital due to holiday hand decorating when you're stringing those lights and stay jolly and injury-free!

True or False Mazes: Christmas ✦ By Scott Peters

TRUE OR FALSE?

Mariah Carey wrote "All I Want for Christmas Is You" in 15 minutes.

TAKE A WILD GUESS! T☐ F☐

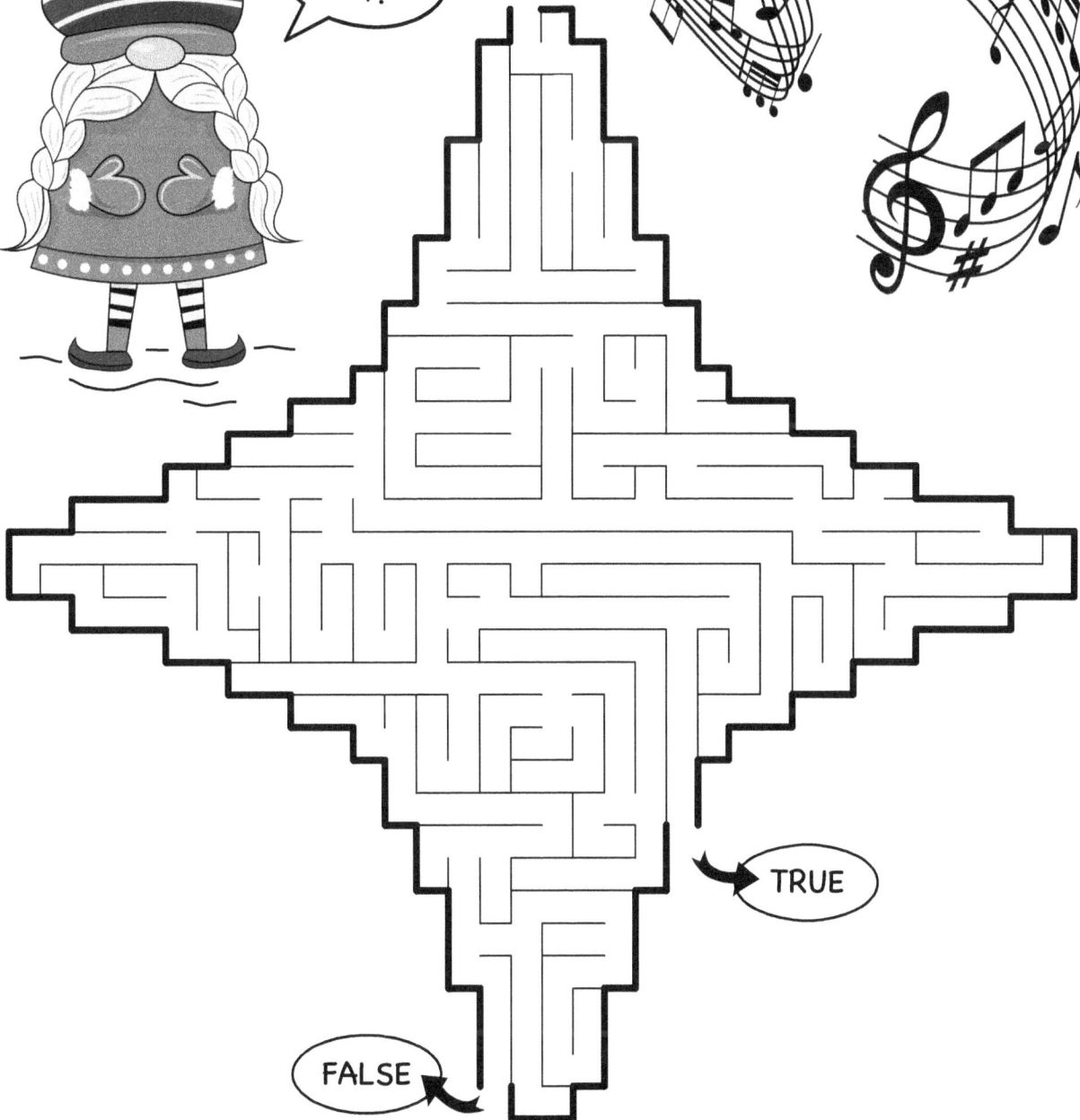

Mariah Carey, penned her holiday hit, "All I Want for Christmas Is You," in just 15 minutes. Her collaborator, Walter Afanasieff, explained to Billboard, "That's why it's so popular—because it's so simple and paldtable."

TRUE OR FALSE?

Santa eats over 300 million cookies on Christmas Eve.

TAKE A WILD GUESS! T ☐ F ☐

EXTRA HARD!

FIND OUT!

TRUE

FALSE

Santa sure has a sweet tooth! Since he visits over 500 million homes and takes a few bites of a cookie at each, he's munching on approximately 335,150,386 cookies. That's a lot of delicious treats!

True or False Mazes: Christmas   By Scott Peters

TRUE OR FALSE?

The X in X-mas is a shortcut someone made up.

TAKE A WILD GUESS! T ☐ F ☐

FIND OUT!

FALSE

TRUE

The "X" in X-Mas isn't just a shortcut—it has a meaningful history! It represents the Greek letter "Chi," which stands for "Christ" in Greek. So, when people write X-Mas, they're still referring to Christ. It's a clever way to respect the birth of Jesus Christmas and the celebration of the holiday's religious roots while keeping things a bit shorter.

TRUE OR FALSE?

Krampus is a scary European Christmas tradition.

TAKE A WILD GUESS! T☐ F☐

FIND OUT!

TRUE

FALSE

Krampus is like Santa's mischievous counterpart. In some central European traditions, he's a hairy, horned creature who roams the streets during the Christmas season. Instead of bringing gifts, Krampus looks for children who've been naughty. He carries chains and bells, making him quite a spooky sight. But don't worry, it's all in good fun, and he's a reminder for kids to stay on Santa's nice list!

TRUE OR FALSE?

Santa is a guest at Macy's Thanksgiving Parade.

TAKE A WILD GUESS! T☐ F☐

FIND
OUT!

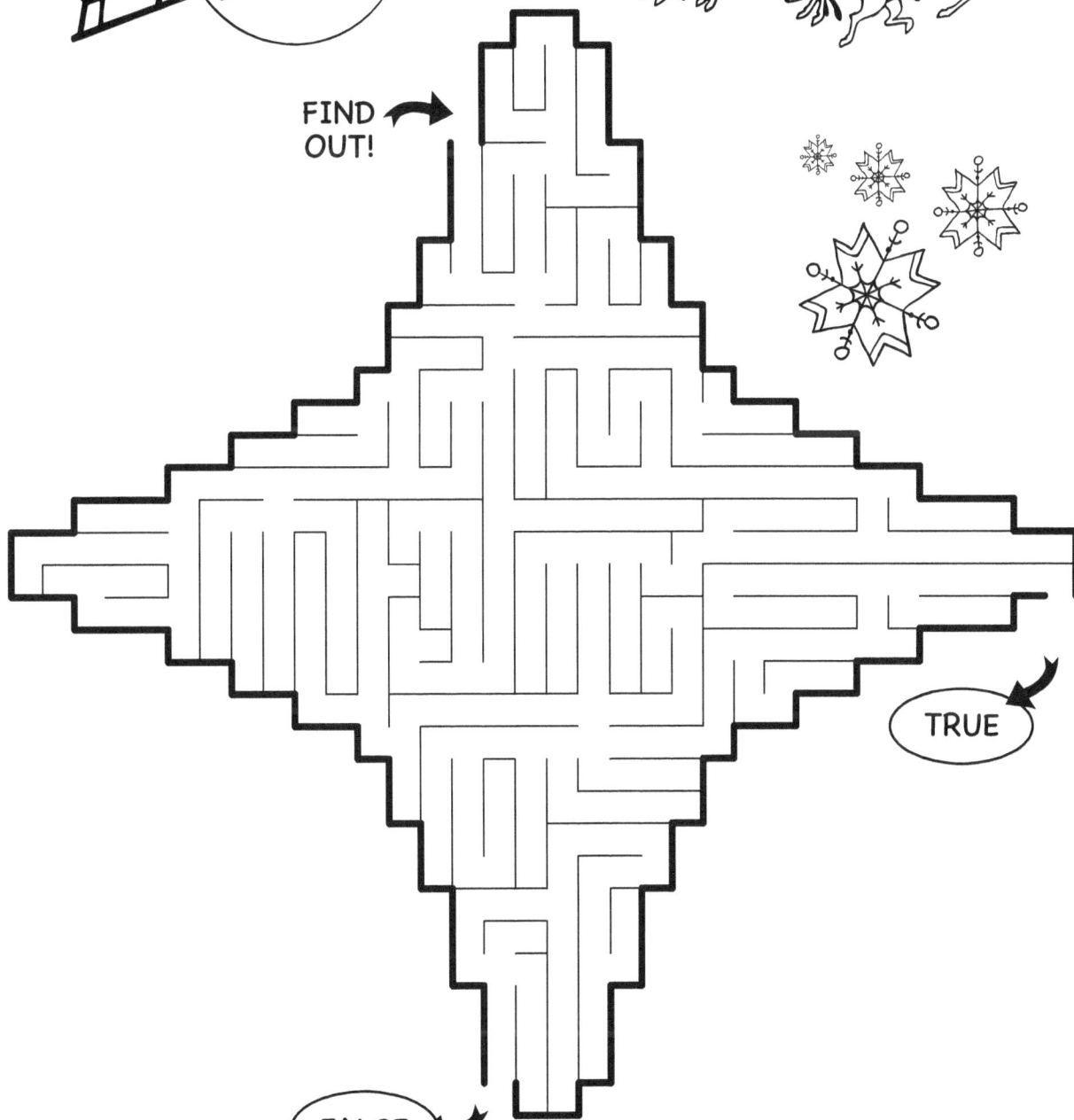

TRUE

FALSE

True or False Mazes: Christmas 💡 By Scott Peters

TRUE OR FALSE?

Rudolph's nose is the only light on Santa's sleigh.

TAKE A WILD GUESS! T ☐ F ☐

FIND OUT!

EXTRA HARD!

FALSE

TRUE

Rudolph's nose shines brilliantly and is the only light Santa uses to find his way. Some folks say it's as bright as a regular flashlight, while others claim it's half as radiant as the sun. Since we've never actually seen Rudolph's nose, we can't say for sure how bright it is. But if you spot a red glow outside your window on Christmas Eve, well, it just might be Rudolph guiding Santa's way!

True or False Mazes: Christmas   By Scott Peters

Page 1

Page 3

Page 5

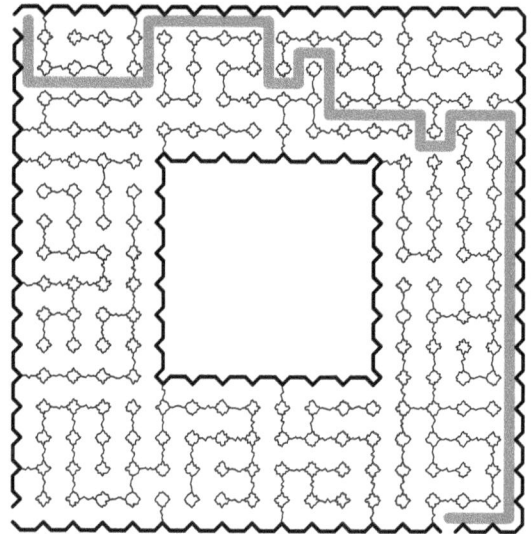

Page 7

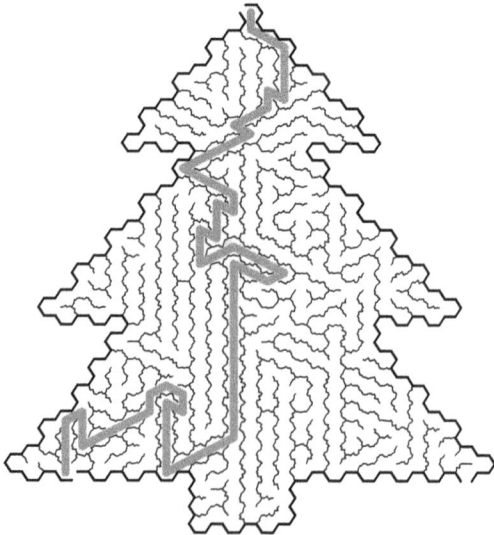

Page 9

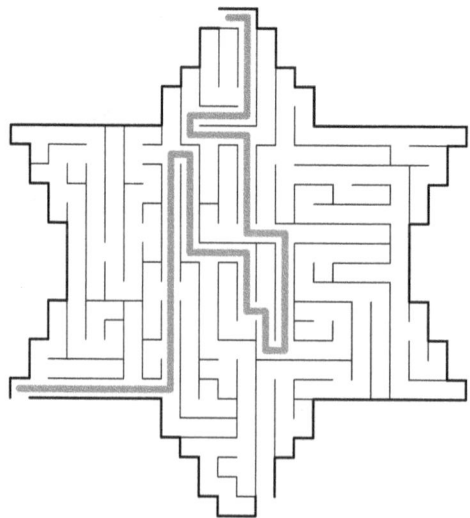

Page 11

Page 13

Page 15

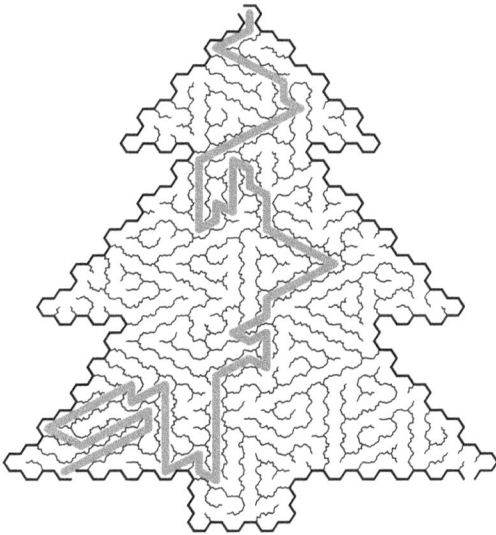

Page 17

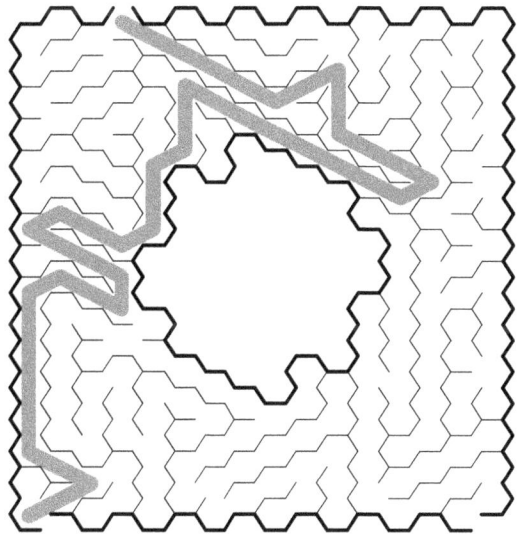

Page 19

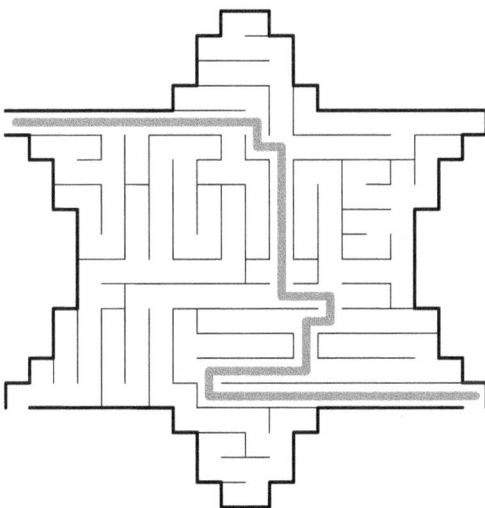

Page 21

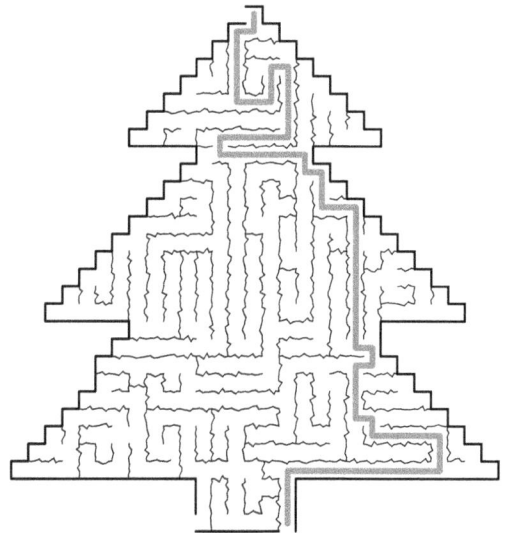

Page 23

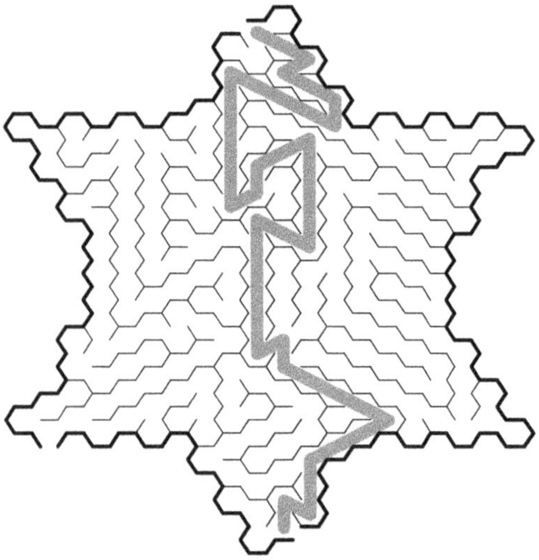

Page 25

Page 27

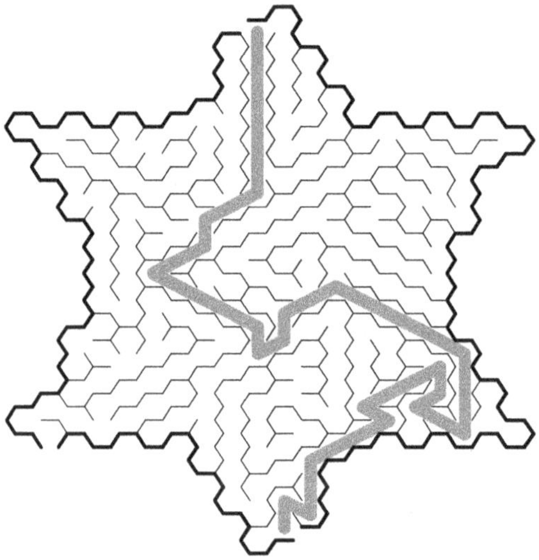

Page 29

Page 31

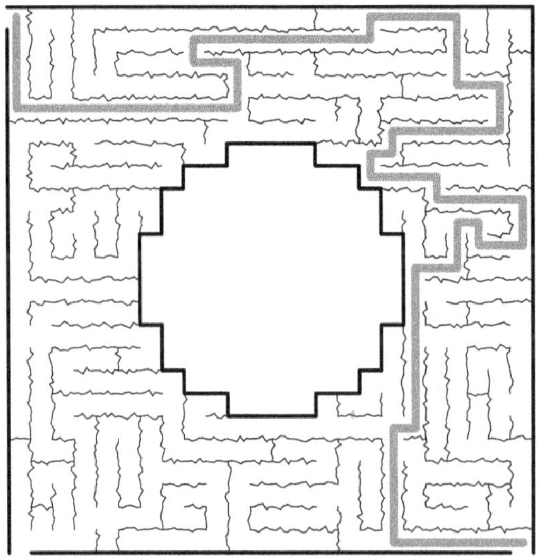

Page 33

Page 35

Page 37

Page 39

Page 41

Page 43

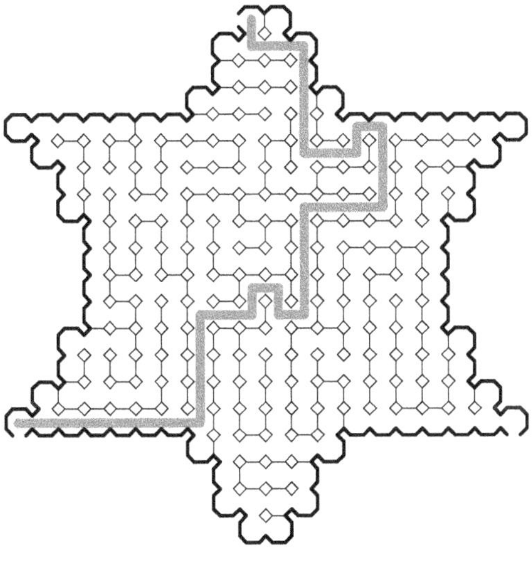

Page 45

Page 47

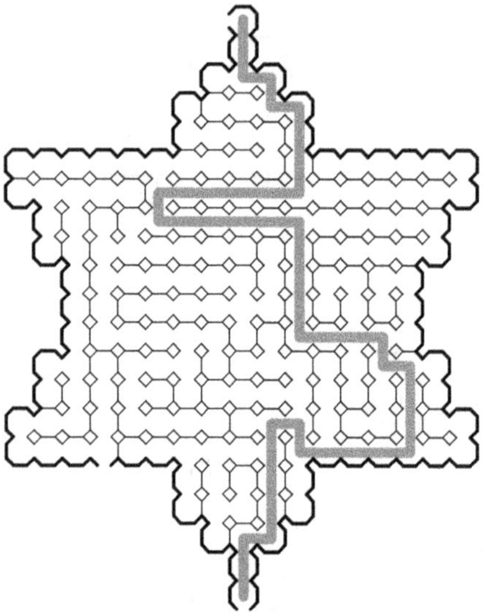

Page 49

Page 51

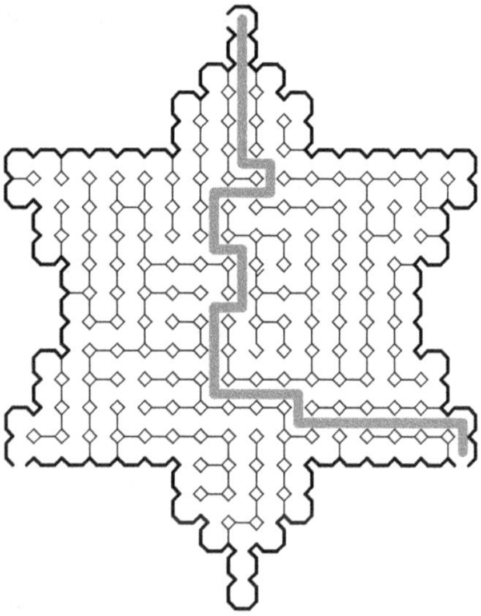

Page 53

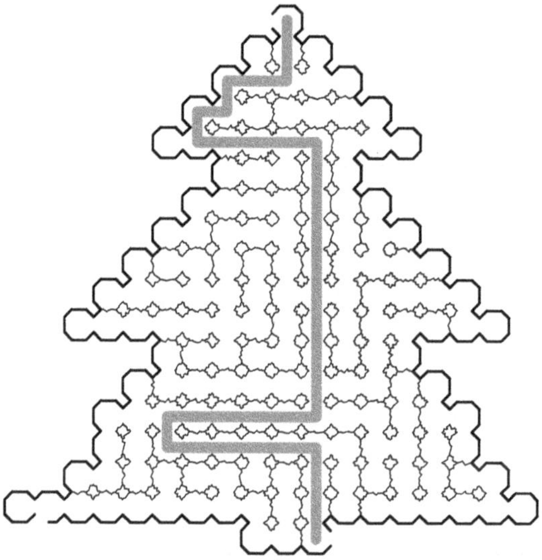

Page 55

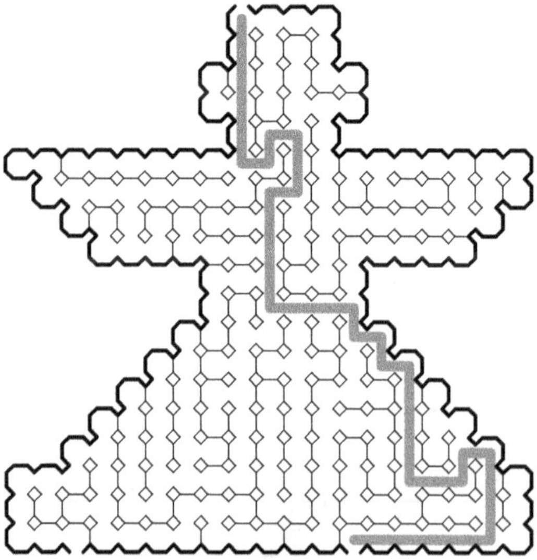

Page 57

Page 59

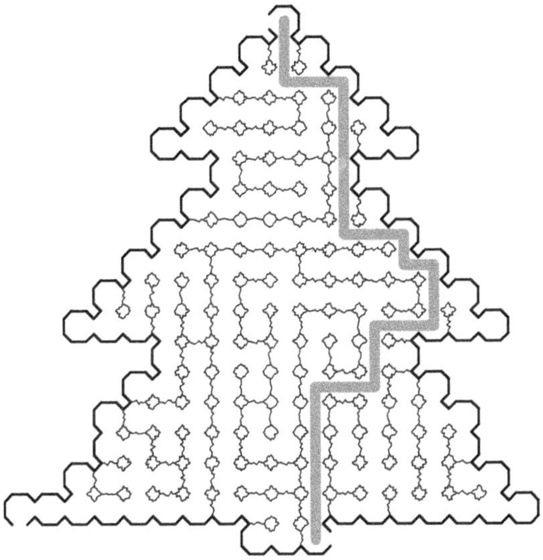

Page 61

Page 63

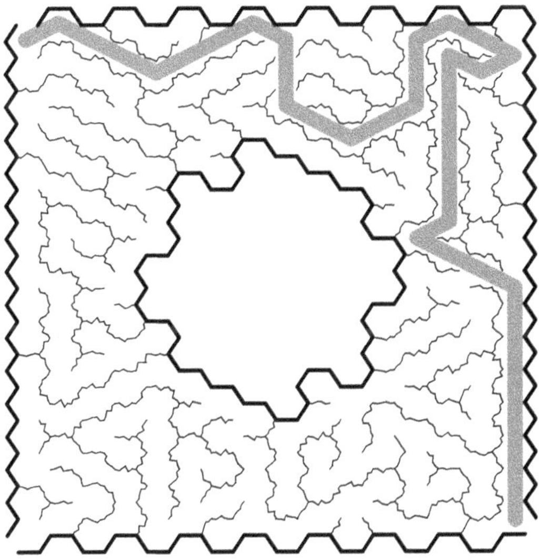

Page 65

Page 67

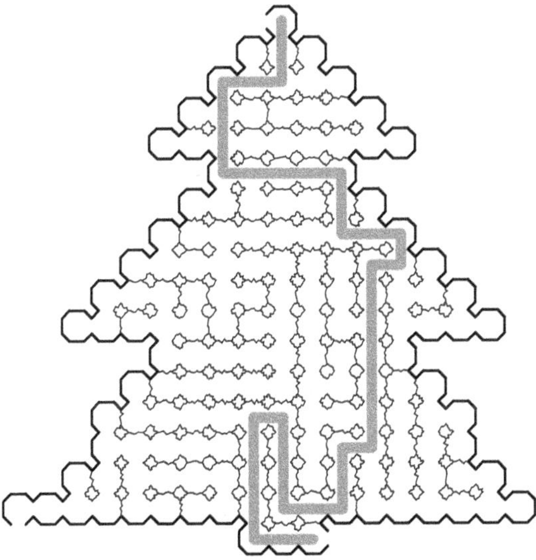

Page 69

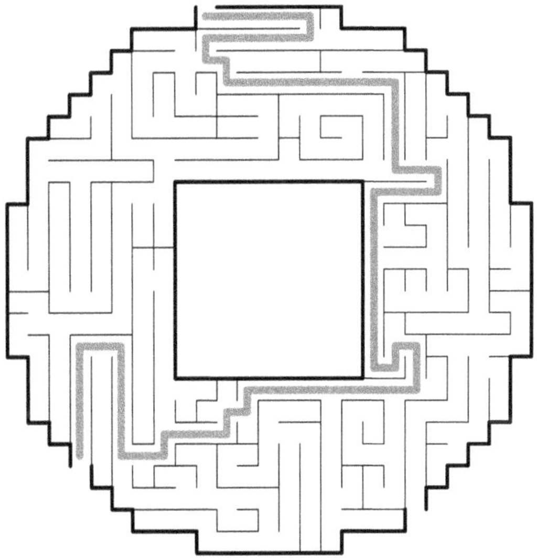

Page 71

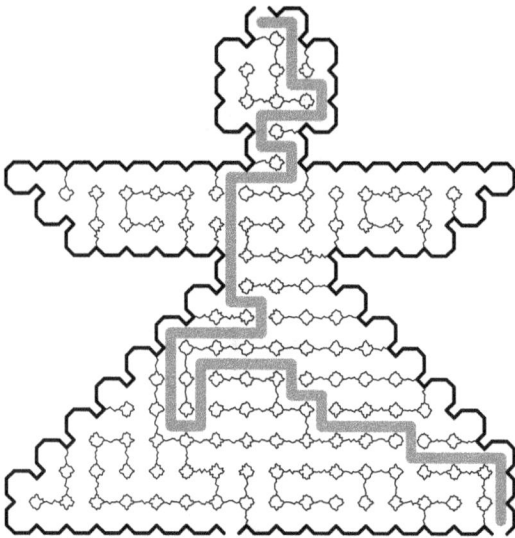
Page 73

Page 75

Page 77

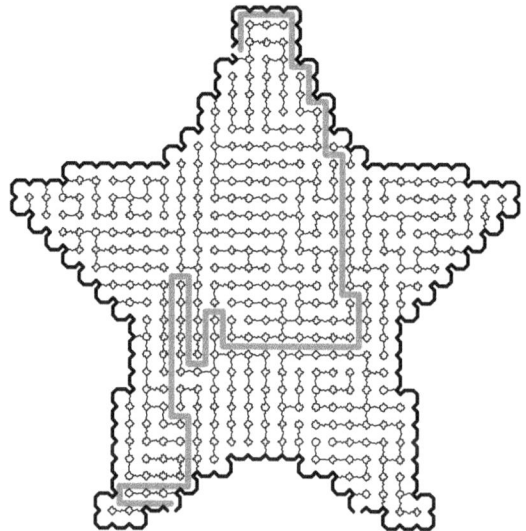
Page 79

Page 81

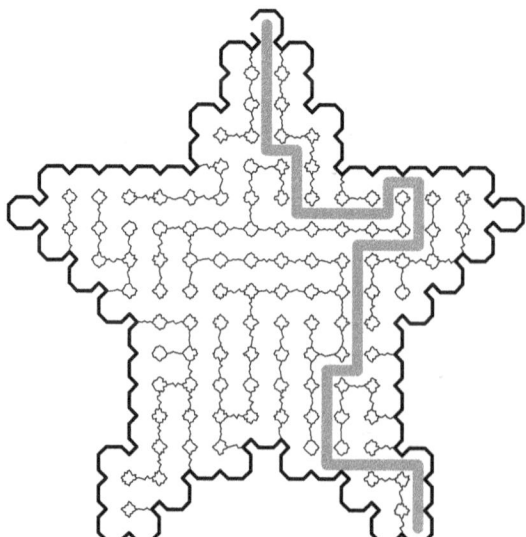
Page 83

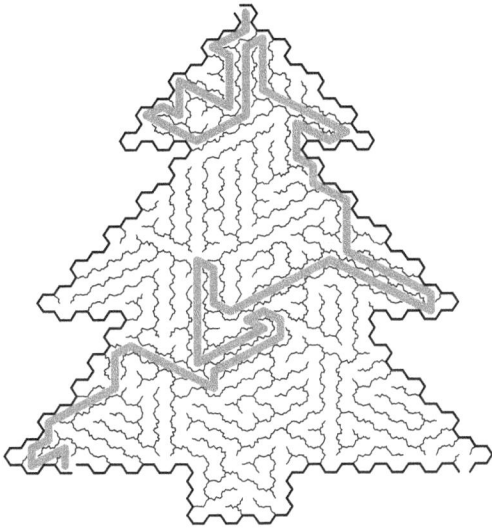

Page 85

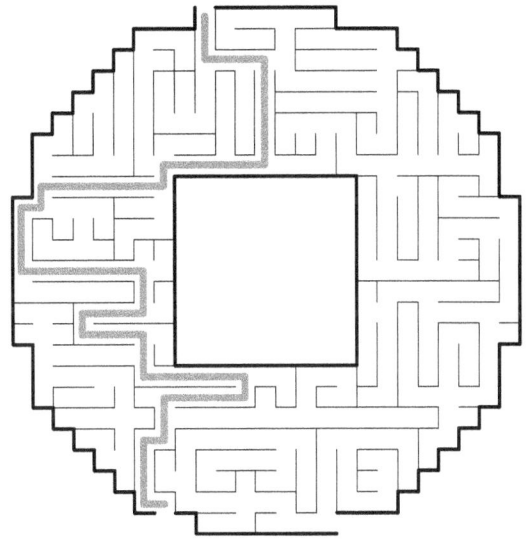

Page 87

Page 89

Page 91

Page 93

Page 95

Page 97

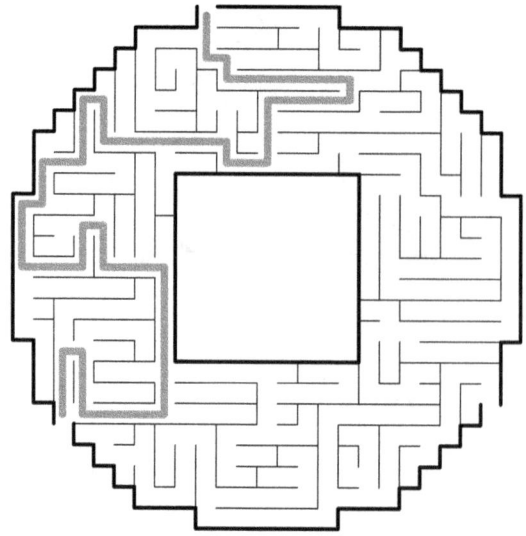

Page 99

Page 101

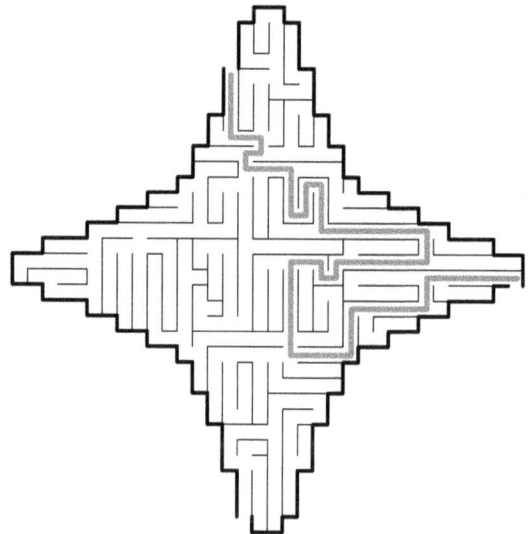

Page 103

Page 105

THANKS FOR PLAYING

The fun doesn't have to end.
Leave a review to help others discover and join in on the excitement.

Happy Holidays!

MORE BOOKS BY SCOTT PETERS

Wacky Facts 50 States Word Search

Clever Kids US Presidents Word Search

Ancient Egypt Activity Book For Kids

The Kid Detective Zet Series

The I Escaped Series

JOIN THE I ESCAPED CLUB

Get a free pack of mazes and word finds to print and play!

https://www.subscribepage.com/escapedclub